FEMINIST FELTIES

FEMINIST FELTIES

21 INSPIRING AND EMPOWERING PROJECTS IN FELT AND FABRIC

Missy Covington

LARK
New York

LARK

New York

An Imprint of Sterling Publishing Co., Inc.
1166 Avenue of the Americas
New York, NY 10036

LARK and the distinctive Lark Crafts logo are
registered trademarks of Sterling Publishing Co., Inc.

© 2018 Toucan Books Ltd.

ISBN 978-1-4547-1075-2

Distributed in Canada by Sterling Publishing Co., Inc.
c/o Canadian Manda Group, 664 Annette Street
Toronto, Ontario M6S 2C8, Canada

For information about custom editions, special sales, and premium
and corporate purchases, please contact Sterling Special Sales
at 800-805-5489 or specialsales@sterlingpublishing.com.

Manufactured in China

2 4 6 8 10 9 7 5 3 1

sterlingpublishing.com
larkcrafts.com

Principal photography by Missy Covington
Design by Leah Germann

Additional picture credits—see page 125

CONTENTS

INTRODUCTION

MY FEMINIST CRAFT JOURNEY STARTED WITH A DUMPSTER FIRE—or to tell the truth, a felt representation of a dumpster fire. In 2016, a number of my favorite authors and musicians died, the political landscape was disheartening, and by the end of the year a common theme with myself and my friends was that 2016 was awful across the board. I had been making felt crafts for my toddler for a while, and when someone posted a Christmas ornament of a 2016 dumpster fire on social media, and asked if I could make one for them, I endeavored to design my own pattern.

I found that spending the wee hours of the night stitching together something that showed my solidarity with others was calming and invigorating. It focused and strengthened my resolve. I wondered what else I could make. I wanted to give felt—a normally innocuous, friendly, fuzzy material—an edge. I wanted to make crafts with themes and details, and a subversiveness that I couldn't find online.

I started with women I admired and branched out into feminist figures and symbols. When the Women's March planned for Washington inspired marches around the world at the beginning of 2017, the pink pussy hat became a symbol of feminist resistance. It became clear that big, vocal protests could be accompanied by quiet, subversive crafting. There was power in needle and thread.

For this book, I have included a variety of items, including personal accessories, sartorial statements, and gifts with an edge. The symbolism and figures in the projects range from modern to historical and (sometimes) ancient, from pussy hats to equality signs, notorious influencers to suffragette symbols and goddesses. Some are tongue-in-cheek, but are also designed to prompt a wry smile. You can make the projects with friends, create them for display, or give something to your grandmother. There is something for everyone, and something to fortify your own resistance moving forward.

MISSY COVINGTON

CHAPTER 1

TOOLS & TECHNIQUES

The projects in this book range from easy to intermediate. But don't worry, the intermediate projects in this book just require some more stitching and patience, not advanced techniques. This first chapter will familiarize you with the tools and materials you need for the projects. It will also outline the basics of working with patterns, gluing, and stitching, as well as show you how to sew the stitches used in the book through step-by-step photos.

TOOLS AND MATERIALS

You will need a range of basic craft and sewing supplies to complete the projects in this book. They are readily available at craft stores, fabric stores, or online retailers.

FABRIC SCISSORS

Sharp fabric scissors are crucial for cutting felt, which can get fuzzy at the edges when cut with a dull blade.

PAPER SCISSORS

Craft or paper scissors are essential for cutting out the paper pattern pieces once you've traced or copied them. Do not use fabric scissors to cut paper—it will dull your fabric scissors very quickly!

HOT GLUE GUN AND HOT GLUE STICKS

Hot glue is superior to other types of fabric glue as it holds felt securely and has an extremely fast drying time. I prefer high-temperature hot glue guns as they allow you slightly more time to work with or reposition your felt pieces before the glue sets.

ACRYLIC FELT

The acrylic felt used in these projects is medium weight and soft. It is available in either bolts or sheets. See page 12 for more details on felt, and page 14 for information about measuring and cutting it.

EMBROIDERY NEEDLES

Embroidery needles come in a variety of sizes, and you can buy several sizes in one package. You'll need various sizes as some of the detail work, such as the stitching for the faces, uses fewer strands of embroidery floss and therefore requires a finer needle; more strands of embroidery floss require a larger eye and therefore a larger needle. A 5/10 variety pack of embroidery needles should provide all the sizes you need.

Embroidery needle

Glue gun

Squares of felt

EMBROIDERY FLOSS

Embroidery floss is made from acrylic or cotton thread, and sold in small skeins. The floss is comprised of six individual threads, which are twisted together. You will use a range of thread strands depending on the project. When you need to pull the threads apart, cut a length of floss the length of your forearm (any longer and it may knot as you use it).

Starting at the center of the length of floss, carefully separate the threads into the number required and then slowly pull the groups of thread apart.

TWEEZERS

A pair of tweezers comes in handy when positioning very small pieces of felt and can save your fingertips when hot-gluing pieces together. I prefer to use very fine-point, curved-tip tweezers.

STICKY TAPE

Taping the pattern pieces to the felt is optional, but it makes it easier to cut out precise shapes. I use matte "invisible" tape, as it is easier to stitch through when adding details.

PAPER

You will need to trace or copy your pattern pieces onto paper. Standard copy paper will work well, but you can also use tracing or pattern paper, if desired. Avoid heavier-weight paper as it is difficult to trace or stitch through when adding details. See page 16 for more about copying and enlarging the pattern pieces in this book.

Fine-point, curved-tip tweezers

Matte "invisible" tape

Embroidery floss

CHOOSING AND USING <u>FELT</u>

Felt is an incredibly versatile craft material. Depending on its thickness, stiffness, and fiber composition, it lets you add fine detail, make sturdy items, and more.

WOOL OR ACRYLIC FELT?

Felt is easy to cut, glue, and sew, and it does not fray. It is available in natural wool fibers or synthetic acrylic fibers. Both have advantages and disadvantages.

Wool felt tends to be thicker, have denser fibers, and a more luxe feel. Wool is naturally water resistant, although it can shrink and cannot be submerged in water and washed without damage. Wool is suitable for fashion projects and items that require denser, thicker felt but don't need fine detail stitching. (The Suffragette Purse on page 68 would be a good wool felt project.)

Felt is available in a range of colors and thicknesses. Thick, acrylic felt is used for the projects in this book.

Acrylic felt is the most common type of felt sold in craft stores, and is available in both single sheets and by the yard or meter.

Acrylic felt has a variety of densities and thicknesses, and won't shrink when washed. Acrylic felt is a good all-purpose material, and is a more economical choice. As such, it's a good material for beginners.

STIFF OR SOFT FELT?

Acrylic felt comes in a variety of fiber densities and treatments, which results in various levels of flexibility.

Stiff felt has been compressed or treated to make it less flexible. Stiff felt has less fiber flyaway and is fantastic for rendering very fine cutout details (like lettering or small intricate objects). However, it is unforgiving of imprecise cuts and can be more difficult to sew through for fine stitch detailing.

Soft felt has more flexibility and a looser density. It's the standard, all-purpose felt that you find in bolts and sheets in craft stores. Its edges are forgiving, and it can be used to render fine stitch detailing quite easily.

Manufacturer variations cause some felt types (or colors within the same type) to become very loose and soft. They are subject to fiber flyaways and imprecise edges. However, very soft felt can be good for filling, cushioning, or as a base for hook and loop fasteners.

THIN OR THICK FELT?

Thin felt (1 mm-thick) is typically stiff. This is useful to know if you're ordering online. Thin felt can be good for making multiple layers without creating an exaggerated three-dimensional effect, or for fine detailing.

Thick felt (1.25 mm-thick) is used in this book and what you'll find in most craft stores. Thick felt provides appropriate bulk and density to support most projects that need a bit of heft. However, interfacing or support may be needed for larger objects (see page 14). Felt of this thickness is also very amenable to layering and sewing detail.

Ultra-thick felt (1.5 mm-thick), if dense, can be difficult to sew through, but it can be extremely durable and suitable for projects that require a bit more stiffness. Wool is often available in ultra-thick or premium densities.

Ultra-thick acrylic felt is not as dense as wool nor does it provide the sturdiness of wool, but it can still be used on projects or areas which will receive a lot of wear such as the bases of purses.

SPECIALTY FELT

You can find stiff or soft felt that has been printed with patterns. Patterned felt typically only has a design on one side of the felt, so keep that in mind when creating pieces where both sides may show.

USING DIFFERENT FELT TYPES

The felt used and pictured in this book is all acrylic, thick, and standard softness. If you wish to experiment with different thicknesses and diverse felt fibers, here are some best uses for alternative types of felt:

- Faces and lettering can be rendered in thin, stiff felt.

- Purses, clutches, bracelets, and hair accessories can be made using wool felt of a higher density and thickness.

Patterned felt is only patterned on one side.

MEASURING & CUTTING FELT

Felt is a very easy material to work with, and it doesn't come with a lot of the drawbacks that other materials might. However, there are a few useful tips to know before you begin.

MEASURING

Measurements in this book are given in both inches and centimeters. Do not mix the units when measuring the felt as this will result in the shapes being less precise. In most instances, the measurements for the amount of felt you need are overestimates so that you have enough felt around a pattern piece to provide enough space for taping the patterns and cutting the pieces.

BUYING THE FELT

When you are planning to make a project from this book, you will need to take into account whether you want to buy your felt material in individual sheets—usually 9" x 12" (22.8 x 30.4 cm) or 12" x 12" (30.4 x 30.4 cm) —or by the yard. Felt is available by the yard or meter from sewing and fabric stores or online.

Larger projects (such as the Suffragette Purse on page 68, and Venus Flytrap Pot Cover on page 104) will require felt cut by the yard rather than several sheets.

The measurements given for the felt required on individual projects encompass the total area of multiple small pieces. If a project is comprised of several smaller pieces, you may still be able to use an individual sheet of felt instead of purchasing it by the yard. To determine what is best, cut out the paper templates and arrange them on a spare sheet of felt or a sheet of paper the same size, to see whether they will fit.

USING INTERFACING

Interfacing is a specialty textile which can be attached to the back or wrong side of a piece of fabric to stiffen and strengthen it. If you want to make a felt item (such as the Suffragette Purse on page 68) sturdier, you can reinforce it with interfacing. A lightweight interfacing will also help smaller items keep their shape. Interfacing is optional: The item will still be perfectly functional without it. The interfacing is joined to one side of the felt using an iron set at medium heat.

To use interfacing:

- Cut a piece of interfacing slightly smaller than the piece of felt you want to reinforce.

- Iron the interfacing to the back side of the felt, following the package instructions, then continue to make the item as described in the steps.

CUTTING

Felt does not fray, but cutting a very small piece can leave the fibers susceptible to loosening and falling apart. (The denser the felt, the less of a problem this is.) For the best results keep the following in mind:

• Use very sharp fabric scissors to cut the felt pieces.

• Be careful when removing the tape —you don't want to snag a small piece of felt.

Although you can cut through multiple layers of felt, they are prone to slipping if you do this. Take care that one piece does not end up smaller than its twin piece.

The sticky tape holds the paper pattern in place while you cut it out. Using a sharp pair of fabric scissors will make the task easier and the cuts more precise.

CLEANING AND STORING

Felt is generally easy to care for and moderately durable. It can be used for practical items, but rough use will cause fibers to fly away or mat. To keep your felt pieces in top condition, here's how to clean and store it.

CLEANING

Wool felt should be spot cleaned only using warm water and gentle soap. Air-dry and stretch it to shape.

Acrylic felt may be washed and submerged in water, but handwashing is recommended to preserve the details added to the projects in this book. Use warm water and a gentle soap, but be aware that some fiber flyaway may occur. Acrylic pieces may be dried in a dryer on low heat, though air-drying is preferred.

Pieces made using hot glue should be hand-washed, but take care as it may detach under vigorous agitation.

STORING

These felt pieces are meant to be used, but if you need to pack them away, place them in a plastic resealable bag and store them in a cool, dry place.

Felt is generally color-fast, but different manufacturers will use different dyes, so keeping your felt out of direct sunlight will ensure bright colors for years to come.

WORKING WITH <u>PATTERNS</u>

Due to space limitations, many of the patterns in this book have been scaled down to fit the page. To use the patterns, you'll need to enlarge or transfer them before cutting them out.

BEFORE YOU BEGIN

A note on the relevant page tells you whether the pattern pieces have been scaled to fit the page or placed true-to-size. It also tells you the percentage to increase the size of the pattern.

TRACING

Patterns that have been printed true-to-size can be traced using standard copy paper or tracing paper. Place the book on a flat surface and trace the outline (including any detail lines) onto your paper, using a writing utensil that won't bleed through the paper (pencil, pen, etc.). If you need multiple copies of the same shape, trace it the number of times required.

If you find it difficult to read the pattern through the paper you are tracing it on to, photocopy or scan the page from the book first, print it out, and then tape the copy to a table or window. A bright light behind the pattern will make tracing easier.

COPYING

To use a photocopier to scale up your paper patterns, simply photocopy the page at the noted percentage. Place the book face down and flat on the scanning surface and select the printing percentage on the photocopy machine.

SCANNING

You can use a scanner in the same way as a copier. In this case, you will have an electronic image of the pattern on your computer, and you'll need to make a percentage-increase selection when printing, or open the image in a photo-editing program and adjust it accordingly.

If you have a handheld page scanner, you may scan and then print the pattern—scaling it up via your computer.

USING YOUR PATTERNS

After you've scaled and printed or traced your patterns, cut them out using a pair of paper scissors. Then position them on the felt. Make sure you have a small border of felt about ¼" (5 mm) around each pattern to make cutting out the shapes easier. Hold the pattern in place using sticky tape, and then cut out the pieces following the instructions for the project you are making. When you remove the tape and patterns from the felt, carefully lift one corner of one end of the tape and then gently pull it away from the felt, taking care not to pull the felt out of shape as you do so.

Print or copy the pattern pieces at the correct size and then cut them out before taping them to the felt.

Place the patterns onto pieces of felt, leaving a ¼" (5 mm) border around the edge. Tape them in place before cutting them out.

PATTERN PRINTING HACKS

If you don't have access to a photocopier you can try printing a pattern from a photograph. It is less accurate, but it does work. To use this method, snap a picture of the pattern—holding your book as flat as possible and making sure to hold the camera parallel to the page (and centered). Then open the picture on your computer and print (adjusting the scale as needed), or open it in a photo-editing program and increase the scale in that way.

NOTE ON ENLARGING PATTERNS

When you enlarge the patterns, not all of the pieces may fit on a single standard 8½" x 11" (21.6 x 28 cm) page. You will need to scale up the pieces separately, unless you're using a large-format printer.

GLUING & FINISHING

The projects in this book are assembled using a combination of glue and embroidery stitches. When you have finished stitching, you can hide and secure the thread ends.

USING HOT GLUE

The majority of the projects in this book use a hot glue gun. This offers a quick way to join pieces of felt together, but there are hazards, particularly if you're not used to using a hot glue gun. However, the benefits—great adhesion, rapid setting of the glue, precise placement, permanence, no matting of the fabric—outweigh the risks. Be careful not to burn yourself. As the name suggests, hot glue is hot!

Household hot glue guns have a temperature range of 248°F (120°C) for a low-temperature glue gun and 380°F (190°C) for a high-temperature glue gun. High-temperature glue guns are preferable for these projects as they allow you to reset sections before the glue sets, and

the felt is unlikely to melt at that temperature.

There are some things to remember when using hot glue.

- Hot glue will leave slight "threads" of glue that will need to be peeled off or snipped away once the glue has dried.

- Do not use hot glue on any part of the felt that you're going to stitch through later. It will be very hard to push your needle through the set glue.

Although using embroidery stitches to assemble the projects make them look more polished, they can be almost entirely glued together, if you want to make them more quickly.

A hot glue gun enables you to apply the glue with precision.

HOT GLUE SAFETY

Please refer to the manufacturer's warnings when using a hot glue gun. You should also consider these project-specific safety tips:

- Use tweezers to place the small pieces of felt to reduce the risk of burned fingertips.

- Utilize fingertip covers (available at hobby stores) if you are not confident about your gluing prowess.

- Do not leave your glue gun on overnight.

HOT GLUE ALTERNATIVES

If you do not wish to use hot glue, you may either carefully stitch on the small details, or use another type of glue. A thick PVA glue or fabric glue may be used, but allow time for the glue to dry before you move on to the next project steps.

FINISHING BASICS

You've carefully cut out, stitched, and glued the sections of your project together. Now make sure you make time to finish everything properly. Hiding and securing the ends of the embroidery floss will make sure your finished item looks great and lasts a long time.

TUCKING IN THREAD ENDS

When stitching two layers together, start the seam by inserting the needle between the two layers, rather than from the back of the piece **(A)**. The end of the embroidery strands will be hidden between the felt layers **(B)**. End the final stitch in the same way. It isn't always possible to do this (for example, when adding detail to a single layer), but it works with most multilayered pieces and produces a neater finish.

KNOTTING THE THREAD ENDS

For most projects, the finished stitches are secured by tucking the ends of the embroidery floss in between two layers of felt. You may, however, choose to knot your embroidery floss—either tying the ends of the strands together, or making a knot in a single strand that is substantial enough not to pull through the felt as you sew.

GLUING THE THREAD ENDS

Hot-gluing the ends of the embroidery floss to the back or inside layers of a finished project ensures that they will not pull out or come loose.

If you are not concerned about the look of the back of a piece, the ends can be glued down on the back of your project **(C)**.

For a polished look, when sewing two pieces of felt together, tuck in the ends between the felt pieces and leave a small hole for the nozzle of the glue gun. Squeeze in a small amount of glue and press the pieces of felt together to secure your final stitches **(D)**.

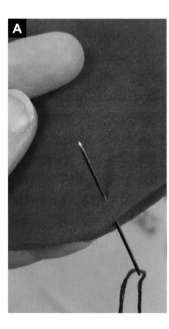

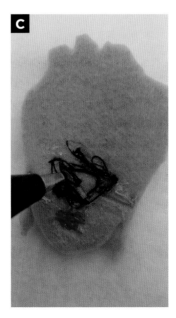

STITCHES

Here are step-by-step guides to all the embroidery stitches you will need to make the projects in the book, from basic joining stitches to more complex three-dimensional stitches for adding details.

STITCHING BASICS

For all the stitches, you will need an embroidery needle and embroidery floss (see pages 10–11). Practice on some scraps of felt first, to perfect the precision and tension of your stitches. Then you'll be ready to start stitching the projects in this book.

Use a piece of floss about the same length as your forearm—any longer and it may tangle as you work. For tips on dealing with the thread ends, see the advice on page 19.

Some projects just use one stitch, while others feature a variety. The stitches used are listed at the start of each design; use this list to check that you are familiar with all the stitches before you begin to sew.

The projects in this book often use more than one stitch. Put your skills to the test with the Labrys Barrettes (see page 120), which use six stitches: backstitch, split stitch, satin stitch, long and short shading stitch, overcast stitch, and running stitch.

RUNNING STITCH

The running stitch is simple and quick, and it gives edges a rustic feel.
The running stitch will, however, pull out if you tug at the end of the thread—be sure not to be overzealous when pulling the thread tight.

1 From the back of the felt, bring the needle through to the front at the point where you want the stitch to begin **(A)**, leaving a tail.

2 Push the needle through to the back of the felt at the desired length of the stitch, then leaving a space the same length, push your needle back up to the front **(B)**.

3 Repeat this process, bringing your needle to the front at the beginning of a stitch and returning it to the back at the end of a stitch, keeping the stitches even **(C)**.

4 The running stitch is used in the Justice Needle Book (see page 54) **(D)**.

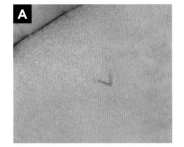

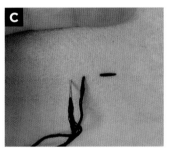

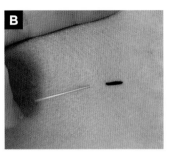

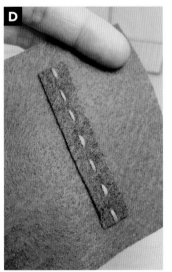

BACKSTITCH

The backstitch produces a smooth, straight line and is the stitch most commonly used for adding detail and securing edges. It will not pull out if you tug at the end of the thread.

1 From the back of the felt, bring the needle through to the front to a point that is a short distance ahead of where you want the stitch to start **(A)**, leaving a tail.

2 Pull the thread through (leaving a tail if this is your initial stitch) and insert the needle at the point at which the stitch should start. Push the needle through from the front of the piece to the back **(B)**.

3 Pull the thread through the back, then place the needle ahead of the next stitch, and bring it through to the front **(C)**.

4 Go back to the end of the previous stitch and, using the same hole, push the needle through to the back. Bring the needle back to the front one stitch length ahead of the existing stitches and repeat steps 3 and 4 to create an unbroken line of stitches **(D)**.

5 The backstitch is used in the Protest Coasters (see page 58) **(E)**.

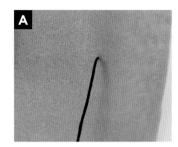

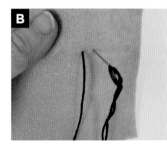

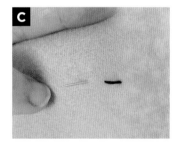

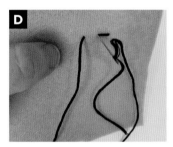

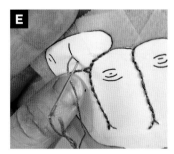

SADDLE STITCH

The saddle stitch is most commonly used for hand-stitched book binding, or for decorative edges. It's a simple stitch that will be very familiar if you've used the running stitch.

1 To start a saddle stitch, begin in the middle of your stitching line. In this example, we'll start from the inside of the object.

2 Bring your needle through the fabric from the front to the back at the point where you want your stitch to begin **(A)**, leaving a tail.

3 At your desired stitch length, bring your needle back to the front **(B)**.

4 Continue stitching in this manner (as you would a running stitch) until you reach the end of your object **(C)**.

5 Begin to stitch to the middle again using a running stitch—you will "fill in" the spaces between the stitches **(D)**.

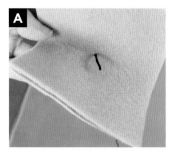

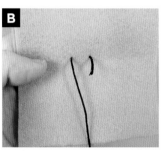

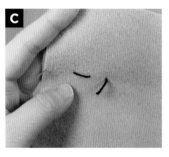

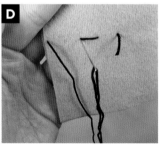

6 Continue to stitch to the other end of the object **(E)**.

7 Reverse the direction of your stitching and continue sewing, filling in the stitches as before, until you return to the middle **(F)**.

8 This example shows how saddle stitch (the yellow stitching) is used in the Justice Needle Book (see page 54) **(G)**.

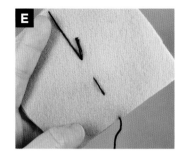

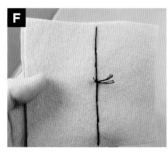

OVERCAST STITCH

This is a simple edging stitch sometimes used to attach inner layers.

1 From the back of the felt, bring the needle through to the front at the point where you want to begin **(A)**, leaving a tail. When joining two layers, insert the needle through just the front layer.

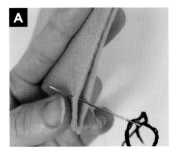

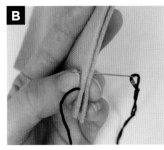

2 Take the needle to the back of the felt and insert the needle back through the felt to the front **(B)**. For small projects this will be about ¼″ (5 mm) along the edge.

3 Repeat the process, inserting the needle from the back to the front every time to create a row of diagonal stitches around the edge **(C)**. Work the stitches at regular intervals.

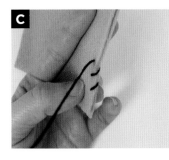

4 This example shows how overcast stitch is used in the Ada Lovelace Egg Cozy (see page 40) **(D)**.

BLANKET STITCH

This edging stitch gives a rustic feel to pieces with a threaded edge. Be sure to keep your stitches even.

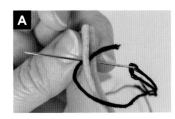

1 From the back of the felt, bring the needle through to the front at the point where you want to begin stitching, leaving a tail, then reinsert it into the back, creating a loop **(A)**.

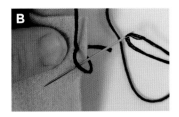

2 Bring the needle through the loop, coming from the outside of the loop and working in the direction you want to stitch **(B)**.

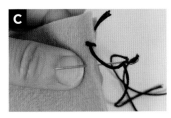

3 Bring the needle from the back to the front, creating another loop at the point where you want to complete the stitch **(C)**. For small projects this will be about ¼″ (5 mm) along the seam.

4 Before tightening the stitch, bring the needle through that loop **(D)**.

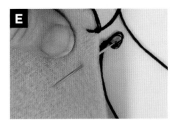

5 Tighten and move onto the next stitch using the same technique **(E)**.

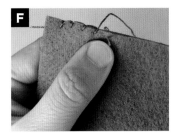

6 This stitch is used in the Justice Needle Book edging (see page 54) **(F)**.

SPLIT STITCH

The split stitch is very close to the backstitch. The difference lies in ending the stitch by "splitting" the previous stitch instead of sharing a hole to create a smooth line. The split stitch creates a more raised, distinct line than the backstitch.

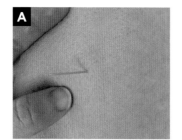

1 From the back of the felt, bring your needle to a point that is ahead of where you want the stitch to start. Pull the thread through **(A)**, leaving a tail.

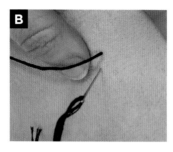

2 Go back to where your stitch should start. Push your needle through from the front of the piece to the back at this point. Pull the thread through to the back **(B)**.

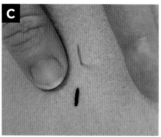

3 Place the needle ahead of the next stitch, and bring it through the front of the felt **(C)**.

4 Bring the needle to the back again by sewing through the previous stitch, splitting the stitch in the middle of the strands **(D)**.

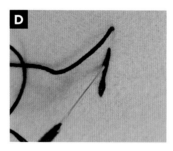

5 The split stitch is used to outline the Labrys Barrettes (see page 120) **(E)**.

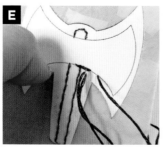

SATIN STITCH

This stitch is good for filling in small areas in embroidery projects. It gives a smooth, flat, even appearance.

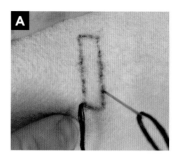

1 Working on a diagonal, bring the needle through to the front of the felt, and down through to the back on the opposite side of the area you want to cover **(A)**, leaving a tail.

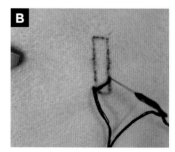

2 Move your needle to the origin point of your first stitch. Bring it through to the front again here, and return to the back at the spot next to the end point of your first stitch **(B)**.

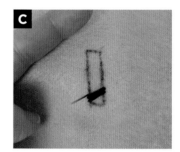

3 Continue stitching until the area has been filled **(C)**.

4 The satin stitch is used on the ax handle of the Labrys Barrettes (see page 120) **(D)**.

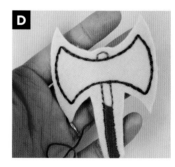

LONG AND SHORT SHADING STITCH

This technique gives the most natural appearance to shading, and is also useful for covering a larger area of an object detail than the satin stitch.

1 At one side of the area to be filled, bring the needle from the back to the front of the felt, just outside the edge of the area. Insert the needle through to the back a short distance away from your starting point **(A)**, leaving a tail.

2 Return to your starting edge, and make another stitch. If your first stitch was long, make this one short (or vice versa) **(B)**.

3 Alternate sewing long and short stitches until you reach the finishing edge of the section to be filled **(C)**.

4 For the next "row" of stitching, randomly alternate sewing long and short stitches, nestling their origin points among the first row of stitches **(D)**.

5 The long and short shading stitch is used on the ax blade of the Labrys Barrettes (see page 120) **(E)**.

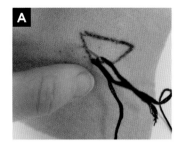

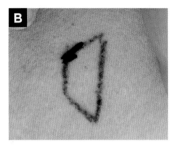

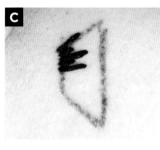

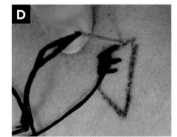

FRENCH KNOT

The French knot is often used for eye details, freckles, flower centers, or any other sort of dots. It essentially creates a fancy, even knot that sits on the top of the fabric.

1 Bring the needle through to the front of the felt just slightly to one side of your desired French knot spot **(A)**, leaving a tail.

2 Keeping the tension even on the strand of thread you've pulled through, loop the thread around the needle twice **(B)**.

3 Keeping the looped thread tight on your needle, hold the slack thread so that it doesn't slip or bunch, and push your needle with the looped strands through the felt at the desired location of the French knot (this should not be the same as the initial hole) **(C)**.

4 Carefully pull the thread through to the back of the felt. The knot will sit on the surface of the felt **(D)**.

5 This stitch is used in the Firebrand Bracelet (see page 50) **(E)**.

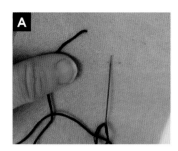

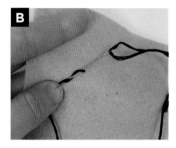

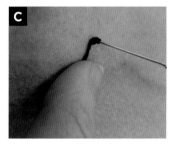

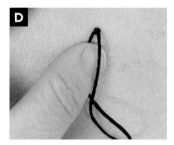

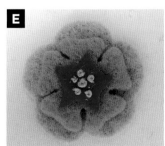

CHAPTER 2

NASTY WOMEN

The women who came before us were trailblazers who used their voices, words, and actions to fight for equality. Their passion and convictions paved the way for the conversations that we have today, and their words and deeds give us strength as we continue the fight—sometimes in the face of what can seen like insurmountable challenges. The women featured in this chapter were revolutionaries, and they continue to inspire us.

BADASS WOMEN BADGE

Wear this badge and take these two icons with you wherever you go. Elizabeth Cady Stanton and Susan B. Anthony were trailblazers in the women's suffrage movement.

YOU WILL NEED

1 piece of dark gray felt, 4" x 4" (10.2 x 10.2 cm)

1 piece of light gray felt, 3½" x 3½" (8.9 x 8.9 cm)

1 piece of cream felt, 7½" x 7" (19 x 17.8 cm)

1 piece of medium gray felt, 2½" x 2" (6.4 x 5.1 cm)

1 piece of black felt, 3¼" x 2½" (8.3 x 6.4 cm)

1 piece of white felt, 3½" x 2" (8.9 x 5.1 cm)

1 piece of dark brown felt, 3½" x 2" (8.9 x 5.1 cm)

Embroidery floss: medium pink, black, dark gray, light gray, dark brown, and cream

TOOLS

Paper scissors

Sticky tape

Sewing scissors

Embroidery needles

Hot glue gun and hot glue sticks

Tweezers

Iron-on adhesive (optional)

STITCHES

Running stitch (page 21)

Backstitch (page 21)

French knot (page 25)

Overcast stitch (page 23)

DIFFICULTY LEVEL

Medium

FINISHED SIZE

3½" (8.9 cm) in diameter

GETTING STARTED

1 Photocopy the pattern pieces on page 31 and cut them out.

2 Tape the paper pattern pieces to the felt, but avoid taping over any stitch detail marks **(A)**:

- The large circle on dark gray felt

- The small inner circle and Susan B. Anthony's brooch on light gray felt

- The main body piece, faces, and hands on cream felt

- Elizabeth Cady Stanton's shirt on medium gray felt

- Susan B. Anthony's shirt and Elizabeth Cady Stanton's fascinator on black felt

- Elizabeth Cady Stanton's hair and brooch, and Susan B. Anthony's collar on white felt

- Susan B. Anthony's hair pieces on dark brown felt

3 Cut out the felt pieces that do not have any marked stitch details.

We both vote in favor!

ADDING DETAILS

4 Add the stitch details as marked on the paper patterns using the number of strands of embroidery floss listed as follows:

- A running stitch in light pink (6 strands) on the light gray inner circle

- A backstitch in black (3 strands) on Elizabeth Cady Stanton's top and the main body piece

- A backstitch in dark gray (3 strands) on Susan B. Anthony's top **(B)**

- A backstitch in dark brown (2 strands) on Susan B. Anthony's hair

- A backstitch in cream (2 strands) for the finger detail on Elizabeth Cady Stanton's hand

- A backstitch (1 strand) in medium pink for the lips, cream for facial lines, black for the eye outline and noses, light gray for Elizabeth Cady Stanton's eyebrows, and dark brown for Susan B. Anthony's eyebrows

- French knots in black (2 strands) for the eye detail on both faces

5 Cut out the detail pieces and remove the paper patterns. You can use hot glue to secure the loose thread ends to the back of the felt so that they don't pull through the fabric when you remove the paper.

FINISHING

6 Use hot glue to join the sections together. Use tweezers to hold the felt as you're gluing and placing pieces in this order:

- Elizabeth Cady Stanton's fascinator onto her hair

- Elizabeth Cady Stanton's hair onto her head **(C)**

- Susan B. Anthony's hair pieces together

- Susan B. Anthony's hair pieces onto her head

- Elizabeth Cady Stanton's brooch onto her top

- Susan B. Anthony's brooch onto her scarf

- Susan B. Anthony's scarf onto her top

- Susan B. Anthony's hand onto her top

- Elizabeth Cady Stanton's top onto the main body piece, aligning her necklace

- Susan B. Anthony's top onto the main body piece

- Elizabeth Cady Stanton's hand onto her top piece

- Susan B. Anthony's head onto the main body piece

- Elizabeth Cady Stanton's head onto the main body piece

7 Use hot glue to attach the light gray circle onto the background circle. Check the placement of the main body piece, making sure it's aligned, then glue it onto the background circles **(D)**.

8 Affix your badge to a bag or coat by stitching an overcast or running stitch with a thread of your choice, or using iron-on adhesive or hot glue.

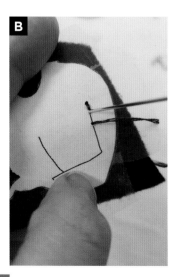

PATTERN PIECES

Patterns shown at 80 percent.
Photocopy at 125 percent to
enlarge them to full size.

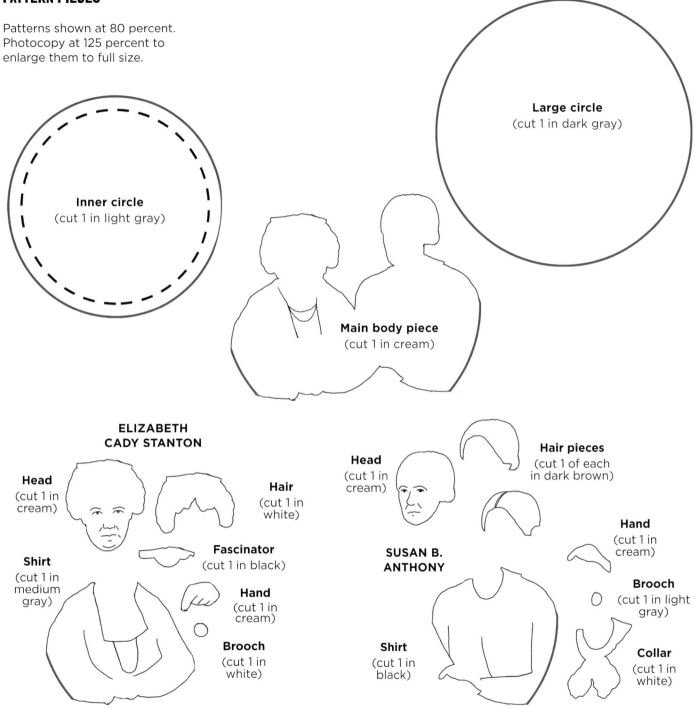

Large circle
(cut 1 in dark gray)

Inner circle
(cut 1 in light gray)

Main body piece
(cut 1 in cream)

**ELIZABETH
CADY STANTON**

Head
(cut 1 in
cream)

Hair
(cut 1 in
white)

Fascinator
(cut 1 in black)

Shirt
(cut 1 in
medium
gray)

Hand
(cut 1 in
cream)

Brooch
(cut 1 in
white)

Head
(cut 1 in
cream)

Hair pieces
(cut 1 of each
in dark brown)

**SUSAN B.
ANTHONY**

Hand
(cut 1 in
cream)

Brooch
(cut 1 in light
gray)

Shirt
(cut 1 in
black)

Collar
(cut 1 in
white)

FIERCE FINGER PUPPET

Pop this Marie Curie finger puppet onto your hand and act out the most radiant scenes. A brilliant chemist and physicist, Marie Curie wasn't afraid to take risks for her work.

YOU WILL NEED

1 piece of white felt, 5" x 4½" (12.7 x 11.4 cm)
1 piece of black felt, 3" x 4½" (7.6 x 11.4 cm)
1 piece of cream felt, 3" x 2½" (7.6 x 6.4 cm)
1 piece of medium brown felt, 1½" x 2" (3.8 x 5.1 cm)
1 piece of light blue felt, 1" x 1" (2.5 x 2.5 cm)
Embroidery floss: medium pink, black, light gray, brown, and cream

TOOLS

Paper scissors
Sticky tape
Sewing scissors
Embroidery needles
Hot glue gun and hot glue sticks
Tweezers

STITCHES

Backstitch (page 21)
French knot (page 25)
Overcast stitch (page 23)

DIFFICULTY LEVEL

Easy

FINISHED SIZE

4" x 3⅛" (10.2 x 8 cm)

GETTING STARTED

1 Photocopy the pattern pieces on page 35 and cut them out.

2 Tape the paper pattern pieces to the felt, but avoid taping over any stitch detail marks **(A)**:

- The back body piece and sash on white felt

- The front body piece on black felt

- The face and hands on cream felt

- The hair on medium brown felt

- The beaker pieces on light blue felt

3 Cut out the felt pieces that do not have any marked stitch details.

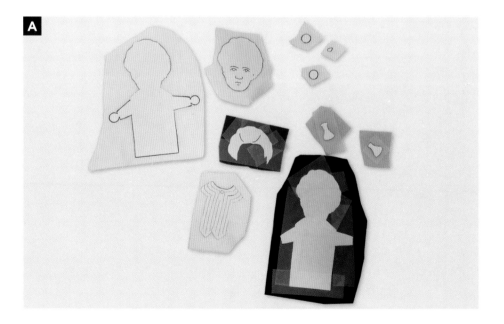

A

ADDING DETAILS

4 Add the stitch details as marked on the paper patterns using the number of strands of embroidery floss listed. Use:

- A backstitch in brown (2 strands) on the hair piece

- A French knot in light gray (3 strands) to add the button detail to the sash

- A backstitch in light gray (2 strands) to add the line detail to the sash **(B)**. Don't stitch the center line.

- A backstitch (1 strand) on the face, using brown for the eyebrows, cream for the ear detail, black for the eye outline and nose, and medium pink for the lips

- A French knot in black (6 strands) for the eyes

5 Cut out the detail pieces and remove the paper patterns. You can use hot glue to secure the loose thread ends to the back of the felt so that they don't pull through the fabric when you remove the paper.

FINISHING

6 Sew the edges of the front and back body pieces together using 6 strands of black embroidery floss and an overcast stitch **(C)**. Be sure to leave the bottom unstitched so you can fit your finger.

7 Use hot glue to attach the additional details to the finger puppet. Use tweezers to hold the felt as you're gluing and placing pieces in this order:

- The beaker pieces together, the smaller piece on top of the larger one

- The hands onto the body

- The beaker onto the hand of your choice

- The thumb next to the beaker

- The hair piece onto the face **(D)**

- The whole head onto the black side of the body piece

- The sash onto the body

Feminist Facts

As a young woman in Poland, Marie Curie couldn't attend university because they admitted only men. Undaunted, she studied in secret. Curie moved to France and became a scientist. She discovered radium, a chemical element that produces radiation. It had gone unnoticed before because it existed in tiny amounts hidden in other minerals. Curie won not just one but two Nobel Prizes; she was the first person to do so! Curie died of aplastic anemia, likely caused by exposure to radiation.

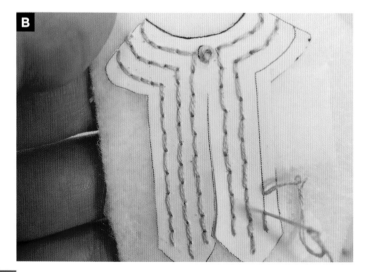

PATTERN PIECES

Patterns shown at 85 percent.
Photocopy at 118 percent to
enlarge them to full size.

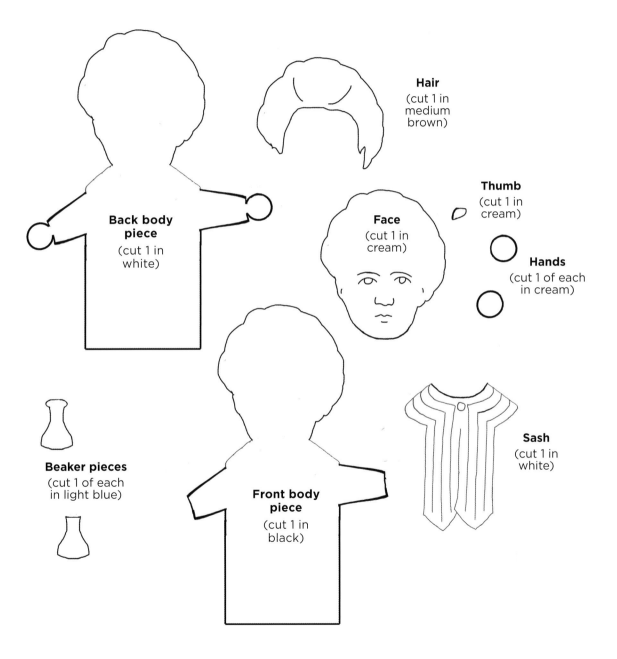

Hair
(cut 1 in
medium
brown)

Thumb
(cut 1 in
cream)

Face
(cut 1 in
cream)

Hands
(cut 1 of each
in cream)

**Back body
piece**
(cut 1 in
white)

Beaker pieces
(cut 1 of each
in light blue)

**Front body
piece**
(cut 1 in
black)

Sash
(cut 1 in
white)

THE BOOKMARK OF TRUTH

Read along with Sojourner Truth: abolitionist, activist, and a strong voice of unequaled power. Take your next journey into a book with her by your side, and stay engaged.

YOU WILL NEED

1 piece of dark blue felt, 9" x 9" (22.9 x 22.9 cm)

1 piece of medium blue felt, 4" x 4" (10.2 x 10.2 cm)

1 piece of light blue felt, 3" x 3" (7.6 x 7.6 cm)

1 piece of brown felt, 7" x 3½" (17.8 x 8.9 cm)

1 piece of dark gray felt, 2" x 2½" (5.1 x 6.4 cm)

1 piece of white felt, 8½" x 4" (21.6 x 10.2 cm)

1 piece of black felt, 3" x 2" (7.6 x 5.1 cm)

Embroidery floss: pink, black, gray, brown, dark blue, and gold (or yellow)

Two 20-inch (50.8 cm) lengths of ⅛-inch (3 mm) wide elastic, or length of your choice

TOOLS

Paper scissors

Sticky tape

Sewing scissors

Embroidery needles

Hot glue gun and hot glue sticks

Tweezers

STITCHES

Backstitch (page 21)

French knot (page 25)

Overcast stitch (page 23)

DIFFICULTY LEVEL

Medium

FINISHED SIZE

Felt disk measures 4" (10.2 cm) in diameter

GETTING STARTED

1 Photocopy the pattern pieces on page 39 and cut them out.

2 Tape the paper pattern pieces to the felt, but avoid taping over any stitch detail marks **(A)**:

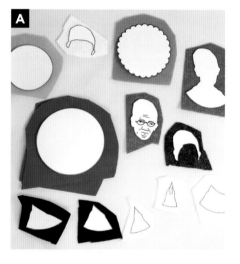

- Two large circles on dark blue felt (cut the first circle, then retape the pattern to the felt, and cut the second circle)

- The scalloped circle on medium blue felt

- The small circle on light blue felt

- The head and body on brown felt

- The hair on dark gray felt

- The base shirt, hat, and scarf pieces on white felt

- The midshirt pieces on black felt

3 Cut out the felt pieces that do not have any marked stitch details.

The truth will prevail!

ADDING DETAILS

4 Add the stitch details as marked on the paper patterns using the number of strands of embroidery floss as follows:

- A backstitch in gray (3 strands) to stitch the detail onto the scarf piece

- A backstitch in black (2 strands) to sew the eyelid, nose, and center lip detail onto the head

- A backstitch in pink (2 strands) to sew the lip detail onto the head

- A backstitch in gray (3 strands) to sew the eyebrow detail onto the head

- A backstitch in brown (2 strands) to sew the facial line detail onto the head **(B)**

- A backstitch in gold (or yellow) (2 strands) to sew the glasses detail

- French knots in black (6 strands) to sew the eye detail onto the head

5 Cut out the detail pieces and remove the paper patterns. You can use hot glue to secure the loose thread ends to the back of the felt so that they don't pull through the fabric when you remove the paper.

FINISHING

6 Use hot glue to join the main body pieces together, starting with the small detail pieces, then moving to the larger pieces to ensure the most accurate placement. Use tweezers to hold the felt as you're gluing and positioning the pieces in this order:

- The head piece onto the body piece

- The hair piece onto the head

- The hat onto the hair piece

- The white scarf pieces onto the black mid-shirt pieces

- The black midshirt pieces onto the white shirt piece **(C)**

7 Position the ends of the two strips of elastic on the back of one of the large dark blue felt circles and glue in place **(D)**.

8 Use hot glue to join the two dark blue circles with the back sides together—be careful to keep the glue toward the center of the circle so you don't have to stitch through it later. Using an overcast stitch and 6 strands of dark blue embroidery floss, stitch the edges of the circles together.

9 Use hot glue to join the scalloped circle to the top dark blue circle, and then the light blue circle to the scalloped circle.

9 Position the body piece against the background. Make sure it's centered. Glue the body piece to the background.

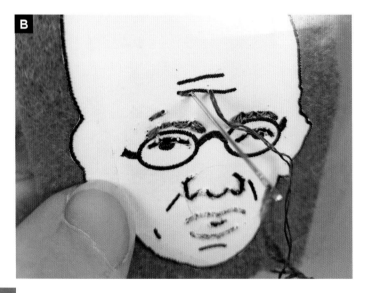

B

C

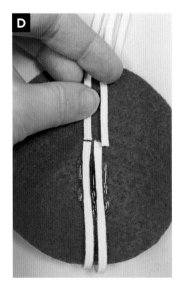

D

PATTERN PIECES

Patterns shown at 50 percent. Photocopy at 200 percent to enlarge them to full size.

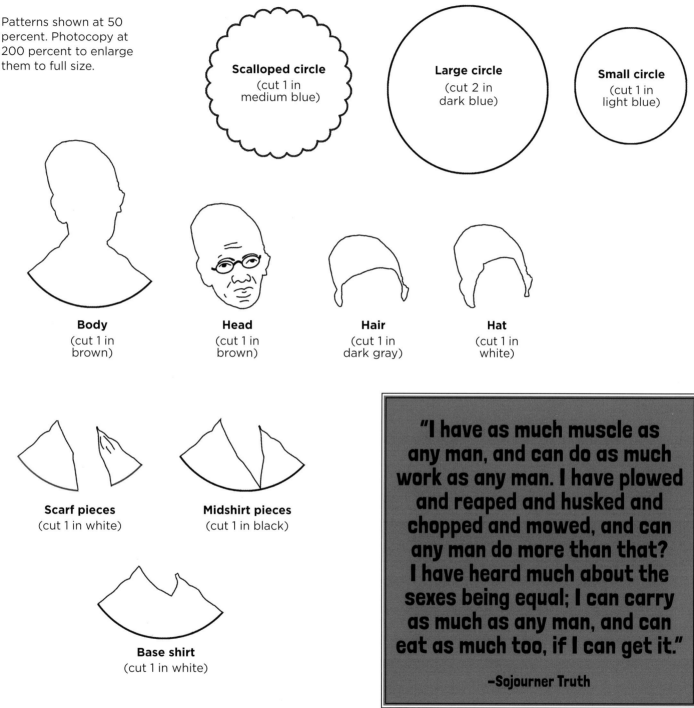

Scalloped circle
(cut 1 in medium blue)

Large circle
(cut 2 in dark blue)

Small circle
(cut 1 in light blue)

Body
(cut 1 in brown)

Head
(cut 1 in brown)

Hair
(cut 1 in dark gray)

Hat
(cut 1 in white)

Scarf pieces
(cut 1 in white)

Midshirt pieces
(cut 1 in black)

Base shirt
(cut 1 in white)

"I have as much muscle as any man, and can do as much work as any man. I have plowed and reaped and husked and chopped and mowed, and can any man do more than that? I have heard much about the sexes being equal; I can carry as much as any man, and can eat as much too, if I can get it."

–Sojourner Truth

ADA LOVELACE EGG COZY

Crack an egg, crack an algorithm. Bring Ada Lovelace—often recognized as the first computer programmer—to breakfast and dine in the presence of a fellow egghead.

YOU WILL NEED

1 piece of purple felt, 4" x 9" (10.2 x 22.9 cm)
1 piece of cream felt, 3½" x 6" (8.9 x 15.2 cm)
1 piece of brown felt, 4" x 10" (10.2 x 25.4 cm)
1 piece of black felt, 4" x 10" (10.2 x 25.4 cm)
1 piece of dark gray felt, 3" x 7" (7.6 x 17.8 cm)
1 piece of white felt, 1" x 2" (2.5 x 5.1 cm)
1 piece of yellow felt, 1½" x 3" (3.8 x 7.6 cm)
Embroidery floss: purple, black, dark gray, brown, yellow, pink, and cream

TOOLS

Paper scissors
Sticky tape
Sewing scissors
Embroidery needles
Hot glue gun and hot glue sticks
Tweezers (optional)

STITCHES

French knot (page 25)
Backstitch (page 21)
Overcast stitch (page 23)

DIFFICULTY LEVEL

Intermediate

FINISHED SIZE

3½" x 5½" (8.9 x 14 cm)

GETTING STARTED

1 Photocopy the pattern pieces on page 43 and cut them out.

2 Tape the paper pattern pieces to the felt, but avoid taping over any stitch detail marks **(A)**:

- The sleeves and two body pieces on purple felt

- The head and arms on cream felt

- Two headdress pieces on black felt

- The hair and buns on brown felt (cut two of the buns)

- The shawl pieces on dark gray felt

- The gloves on white felt

- The fan and flowers on yellow

3 Cut out the felt pieces that do not have any marked stitch details.

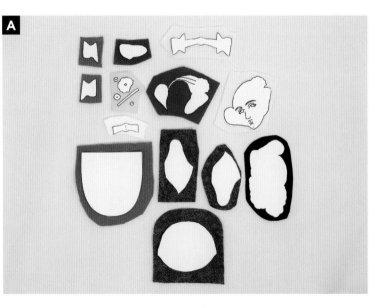

ADDING DETAILS

4 Add the stitch details as marked on the paper patterns using the number of strands of embroidery floss listed as follows:

- A single stitch in black (3 strands) to stitch the finger detail on the gloves

- French knots in black (6 strands) on the four flowers

- A backstitch in yellow (3 strands) to sew the headband detail on the hair

- A backstitch in cream (2 strands) for the facial lines on the chin and above the eye on the head

- A backstitch in black (2 strands) for the nose, medium lip, and eye detail on the head

- A backstitch in brown (3 strands) for the eyebrows on the head

- A French knot in black (6 strands) for the eyes on the head

5 Cut out the detail pieces and remove the paper patterns. You can use hot glue to secure the loose thread ends to the back of the felt so that they don't pull through the fabric when you remove the paper.

FINISHING

6 Place the purple body pieces together, then position the gray shawl sections on the front and back. Sew the side seams together using the overcast stitch and 6 strands of purple embroidery floss for the purple sections and gray for the gray sections **(B)**. Do not stitch the bottom of the body as this will be the opening of the cozy.

7 Assemble the head and headress. Use the overcast stitch and 6 strands of black embroidery floss to join the two headress layers together. Use hot glue to join the hair to the top of the headress; the buns to the hair; and the largest flower to the headress.

8 To complete the body, use hot glue to attach the purple sleeves to each side of the cream arm piece; the white glove to the center of the cream arm piece; and the yellow fan behind the arm piece, as though it were being clutched by the hands **(C)**.

9 Use hot glue to join the remaining pieces together in this order:

- The headress to the top back of the egg cozy **(D)**

- The head piece on the top front of the egg cozy, aligning it with the headress

- The arm piece to the front of the body piece, overlapping the shawl

- The three remaining yellow flowers to the headress

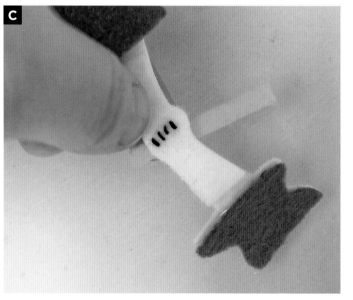

PATTERN PIECES

Patterns shown at 50 percent.
Photocopy at 200 percent to
enlarge them to full size.

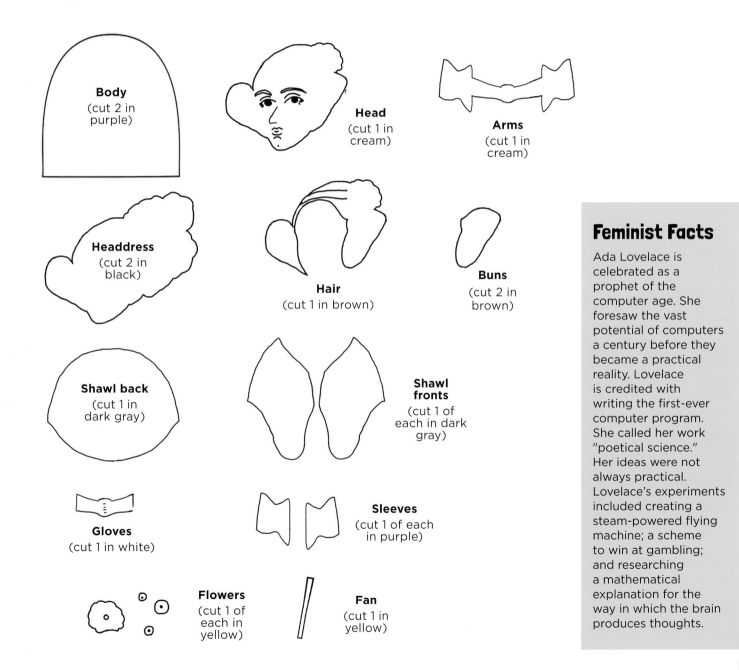

Body
(cut 2 in
purple)

Head
(cut 1 in
cream)

Arms
(cut 1 in
cream)

Headdress
(cut 2 in
black)

Hair
(cut 1 in brown)

Buns
(cut 2 in
brown)

Shawl back
(cut 1 in
dark gray)

**Shawl
fronts**
(cut 1 of
each in dark
gray)

Gloves
(cut 1 in white)

Sleeves
(cut 1 of each
in purple)

Flowers
(cut 1 of
each in
yellow)

Fan
(cut 1 in
yellow)

Feminist Facts

Ada Lovelace is
celebrated as a
prophet of the
computer age. She
foresaw the vast
potential of computers
a century before they
became a practical
reality. Lovelace
is credited with
writing the first-ever
computer program.
She called her work
"poetical science."
Her ideas were not
always practical.
Lovelace's experiments
included creating a
steam-powered flying
machine; a scheme
to win at gambling;
and researching
a mathematical
explanation for the
way in which the brain
produces thoughts.

ROSIE THE RIVETER COIN PURSE

When men went off to fight in World War II, women stepped up. Rosie the Riveter symbolizes their economic power. Use this purse as a reminder of the attitude that continues the revolution.

YOU WILL NEED

1 metal frame purse clasp, approximately 3" x 5" (7.6 x 12.7 cm)

1 piece of navy felt, 10" x 9" (25.4 x 22.9 cm)

1 piece of yellow felt, 4" x 3¼" (10.2 x 8.3 cm)

1 piece of cream felt, 6½" x 7½" (16.5 x 19 cm)

1 piece of brown felt, 1½" x 1½" (3.8 x 3.8 cm)

1 piece of red felt, 2" x 2" (5.1 x 5.1 cm)

1 piece of blue felt, 5" x 5" (12.7 x 12.7 cm)

1 piece of white felt, ½" x ½" (1.3 x 1.3 cm)

Embroidery floss: navy, black, red, and dark brown

TOOLS

Paper scissors

Sticky tape

Sewing scissors

Embroidery needles

Hot glue gun and hot glue sticks

Tweezers

STITCHES

Backstitch (page 21)

Overcast stitch (page 23)

DIFFICULTY LEVEL

Easy

FINISHED SIZE

5" x 5¼" (12.7 x 13.3 cm)

GETTING STARTED

1 Photocopy the pattern pieces on page 47 and cut them out.

2 Since the size and shape of purse clasps may vary, check your paper pattern against your clasp and adjust it accordingly by trimming or extending it as required **(A)**.

3 Tape the paper pattern pieces to the felt, but avoid taping over any stitch detail marks **(B)**:

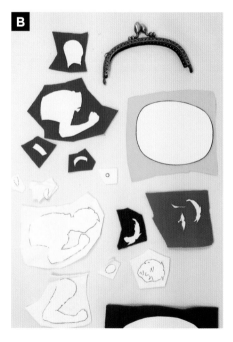

- The two purse sections on navy felt (not shown in the photograph)

- The inner circle on yellow felt

- The body, face, arm, hand, knuckles, and thumb on cream felt

- The hair on brown felt

- The bandanna on red felt

- The shirt, cuff, sleeve, and collar on blue felt

- The collar badge on white felt

4 Cut out the felt pieces that do not have any marked stitch details.

ADDING DETAILS

5 Add the stitch details to the face piece as marked on the paper patterns. Use 2 strands of embroidery floss and a backstitch to stitch as follows:

- Red for the lips
- Black to sew the eye and mouth details
- Dark brown to sew the brows **(C)**
- Cream to sew chin and ear markings

6 Cut out the face piece and carefully remove the paper pattern. You can use hot glue to secure the loose thread ends to the back of the felt so that they don't pull through the fabric when you remove the paper.

MAKING THE PURSE

7 To assemble the purse, use 6 strands of navy embroidery floss and an overcast stitch to sew the side seams of the two navy background pieces together. Only sew the bottom half of the pieces, leaving the top half open for the clasp.

8 Insert the top of one piece of felt into the metal clasp. Stitch through the holes in the clasp and the felt to join them **(D)**. Repeat on the other side of the clasp.

FINISHING

8 Use hot glue to join the main body pieces together, starting with the small detail pieces, then moving to the larger pieces to ensure the most accurate placement. Use tweezers to hold the felt as you're gluing the pieces in this order:

- The collar onto the shirt and the cuff onto the sleeve
- The arm onto the shirt piece
- The shirt onto the main body piece
- The sleeve onto the arm piece
- The hand onto the raised arm and the knuckles on top of the hand
- The thumb piece onto the raised fist
- The second hand onto the shirt
- The bow onto the bandanna
- The bandanna onto the hair
- The hair piece onto the head
- The bandanna side onto the head **(E)**
- The head piece onto the body

9 Use hot glue to attach the yellow background piece onto the center of the purse. Carefully position the figure on the background, then glue it in position.

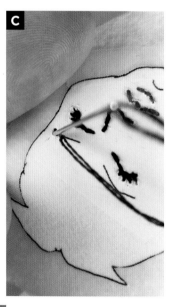

PATTERN PIECES

Patterns shown at 70 percent.
Photocopy at 142 percent to
enlarge them to full size.

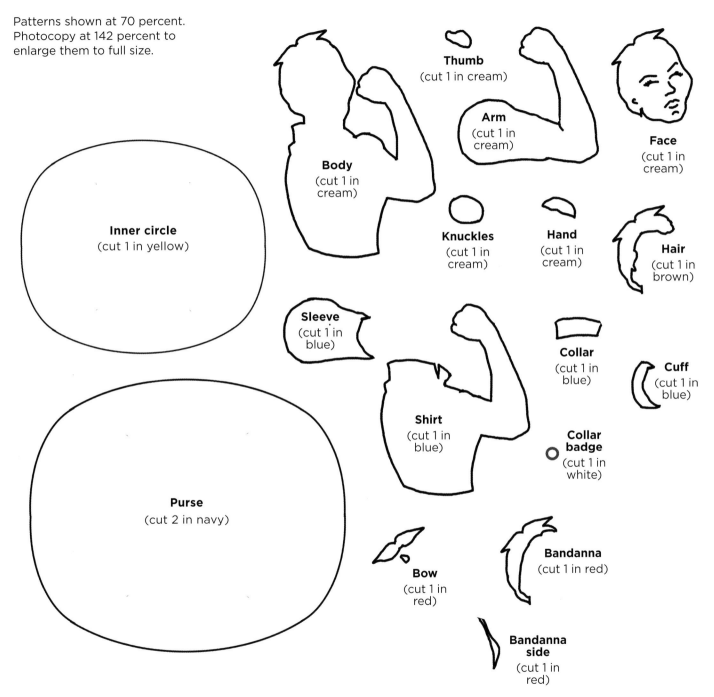

Inner circle
(cut 1 in yellow)

Body
(cut 1 in
cream)

Thumb
(cut 1 in cream)

Arm
(cut 1 in
cream)

Face
(cut 1 in
cream)

Knuckles
(cut 1 in
cream)

Hand
(cut 1 in
cream)

Hair
(cut 1 in
brown)

Sleeve
(cut 1 in
blue)

Collar
(cut 1 in
blue)

Cuff
(cut 1 in
blue)

Shirt
(cut 1 in
blue)

**Collar
badge**
(cut 1 in
white)

Purse
(cut 2 in navy)

Bow
(cut 1 in
red)

Bandanna
(cut 1 in red)

**Bandanna
side**
(cut 1 in
red)

CHAPTER 3

SIGNS OF CHANGE

The feminist movement wasn't born yesterday! For centuries, activists have used symbols and signs to rally others to the cause, using them to give a sly wink to a like-minded neighbor who could not speak up on her own or to show ongoing defiance in the face of setbacks. The symbols and signs in this section range from the simple scales of justice, to the blunt symbol of Venus, to the classic suffragette rose and the raised fist of resistance.

FIREBRAND BRACELET

The symbols and colors used on this bracelet are based on those of the National Union of Women's Suffrage Societies. Wear one as a reminder of the freedom fighters who came before you.

YOU WILL NEED

1 piece of medium purple felt, 2" x 10" (5.1 x 25.5 cm)

1 piece of medium green felt, 2" x 12" (5.1 x 30.5 cm)

1 piece of light purple felt, 2" x 5" (5.1 x 13 cm)

1 piece of burgundy felt, 1" x 2½" (2.5 x 6.4 cm)

1 piece of light green felt, 5" x 5" (13 x 13 cm)

Leather lacing, 12 inches (30.5 cm) long

Embroidery floss: light green

Four ⅛-inch (3 mm) grommets

TOOLS

Paper scissors

Sticky tape

Sewing scissors

Embroidery needles

Hot glue gun and hot glue sticks

Tweezers

Grommet kit and hammer

STITCHES

French knot (page 25)

DIFFICULTY LEVEL

Easy

FINISHED SIZE

1½" x 8" (3.8 x 20.3 cm)

GETTING STARTED

1 Photocopy the pattern pieces on page 53 and cut them out.

2 Tape the paper pattern pieces to the felt, but avoid taping over any stitch detail marks **(A)**:

- The background bracelet piece and middle rose base on medium purple felt

- The foreground bracelet piece, middle rose secondary layer, and two flanking roses secondary layers on medium green felt

- The third middle rose layer, middle rose center, and two flanking rose bases on light purple felt

- The fourth middle rose layer, and two flanking rose centers on burgundy felt

- All the leaves on light green felt

3 Cut out the felt pieces that do not have any marked stitch details.

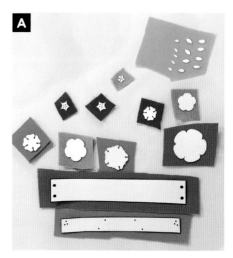

Deeds not words!

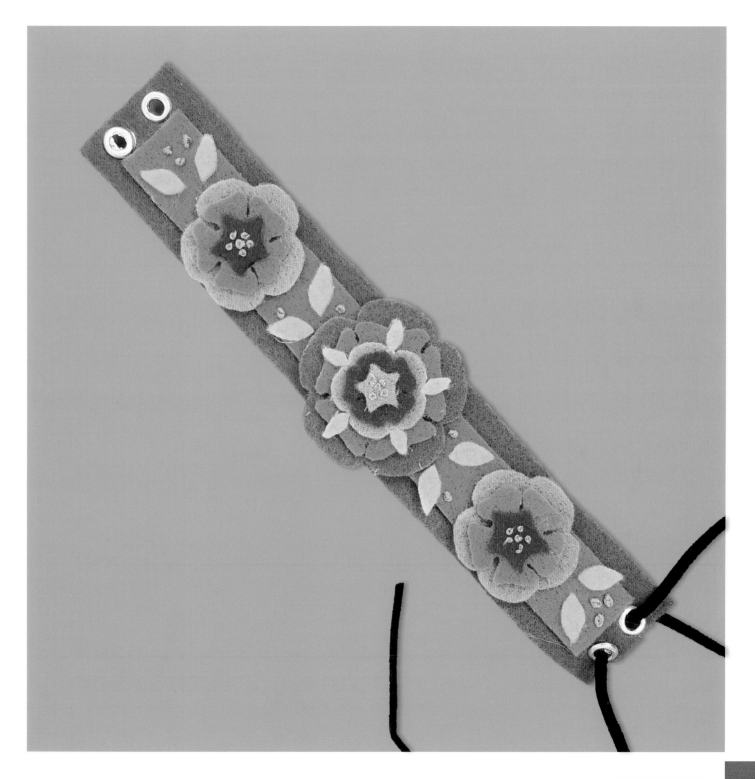

ADDING DETAILS

4 Stitch French knots in light green embroidery floss to add the stitch details as marked on the following paper patterns, using the number of strands listed:

- The foreground bracelet piece (6 strands)
- The two flanking rose centers (3 strands)
- The middle rose center (3 strands)

5 Cut out the detail pieces and remove the paper patterns. You can use hot glue to secure the loose thread ends to the back of the felt so that they don't pull through the fabric when you remove the paper.

FINISHING

6 Use hot glue to assemble the band. Glue the medium green foreground to the medium purple background. Following the marks on the background pattern, cut four small holes (two on either side) into the purple band.

7 Use hot glue to assemble the band detail as follows:

- All five layers of the middle flower **(B)**
- The middle flower to the center of the bracelet
- The leaf pieces to the middle flower
- All three layers of the two flanking flowers together
- The two flanking flowers and the band leaf pieces onto the bracelet **(C)**

8 Following the package instructions, use the grommet kit to affix the grommets to the bracelet and reinforce the holes made in step 6.

9 Thread the length of leather lacing through the grommets, tie in a bow, and trim to desired length **(D)**.

TIP

If you haven't used a grommet kit before, practice attaching the grommets to a scrap of felt to ensure correct placement on the bracelet.

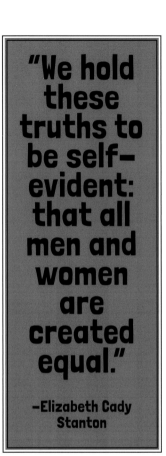

"We hold these truths to be self-evident: that all men and women are created equal."

—Elizabeth Cady Stanton

B

C

D

PATTERN PIECES

Patterns shown at 80 percent. Photocopy at 125 percent to enlarge them to full size.

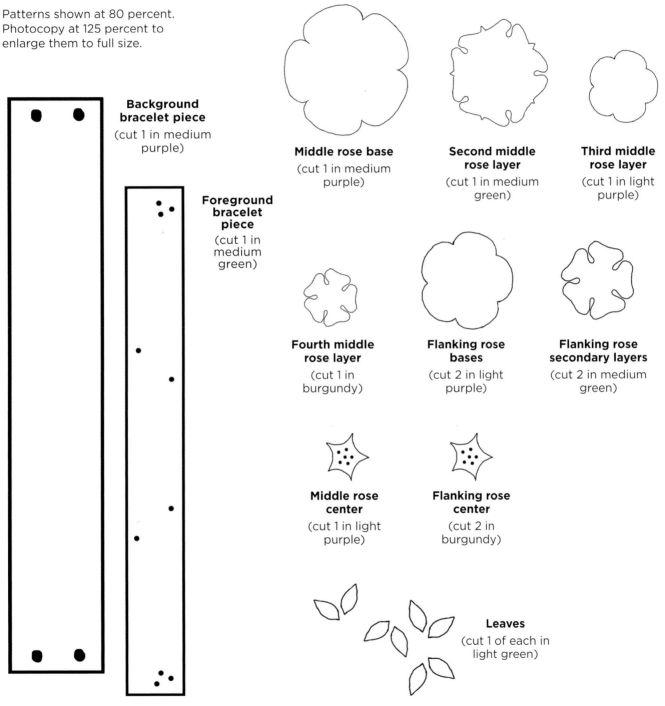

Background bracelet piece

(cut 1 in medium purple)

Foreground bracelet piece

(cut 1 in medium green)

Middle rose base

(cut 1 in medium purple)

Second middle rose layer

(cut 1 in medium green)

Third middle rose layer

(cut 1 in light purple)

Fourth middle rose layer

(cut 1 in burgundy)

Flanking rose bases

(cut 2 in light purple)

Flanking rose secondary layers

(cut 2 in medium green)

Middle rose center

(cut 1 in light purple)

Flanking rose center

(cut 2 in burgundy)

Leaves

(cut 1 of each in light green)

JUSTICE NEEDLE BOOK

In pursuit of justice—through craft or otherwise— you never know when you'll need to engage in a little meditative stitchery. With this needle book, you'll be ready to sew at a second's notice.

YOU WILL NEED

1 piece of teal felt, 6½" x 8" (16.5 x 20.3 cm)

1 piece of patterned felt, 6½" x 8" (16.5 x 20.3 cm)

1 piece of golden yellow felt, 8½" x 3½" (21.6 x 8.9 cm)

1 piece of dark gray felt, 6" x 3" (15.2 x 7.6 cm)

Embroidery floss: dark gray and golden yellow

One 2-inch (5.1 cm) and one 3-inch (7.6 cm) length of thin elastic

1 shank button

TOOLS

Paper scissors

Sticky tape

Sewing scissors

Embroidery needles

Hot glue gun and hot glue sticks

STITCHES

Backstitch (page 21)

Running stitch (page 21)

Blanket stitch (page 23)

Saddle stitch (page 22)

DIFFICULTY LEVEL

Easy

FINISHED SIZE

3" x 3½" (7.6 x 8.9 cm)

GETTING STARTED

1 Photocopy the pattern pieces on page 57 and cut them out.

2 Tape the paper pattern pieces to the felt, but avoid taping over any stitch detail marks **(A)**:

- The cover outer layer and liner on teal felt

- The inner and outer pages on patterned felt

- The scales of justice pieces on golden yellow felt

- The needle pockets and holders on golden yellow and dark gray felt

3 Cut out the felt pieces that do not have any marked stitch details. Keep the paper patterns to use as a guide when assembling the felt pieces.

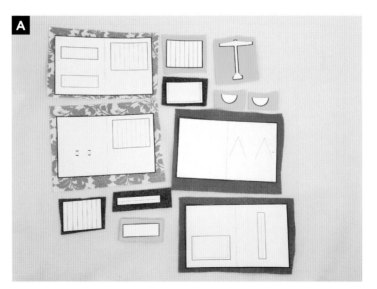

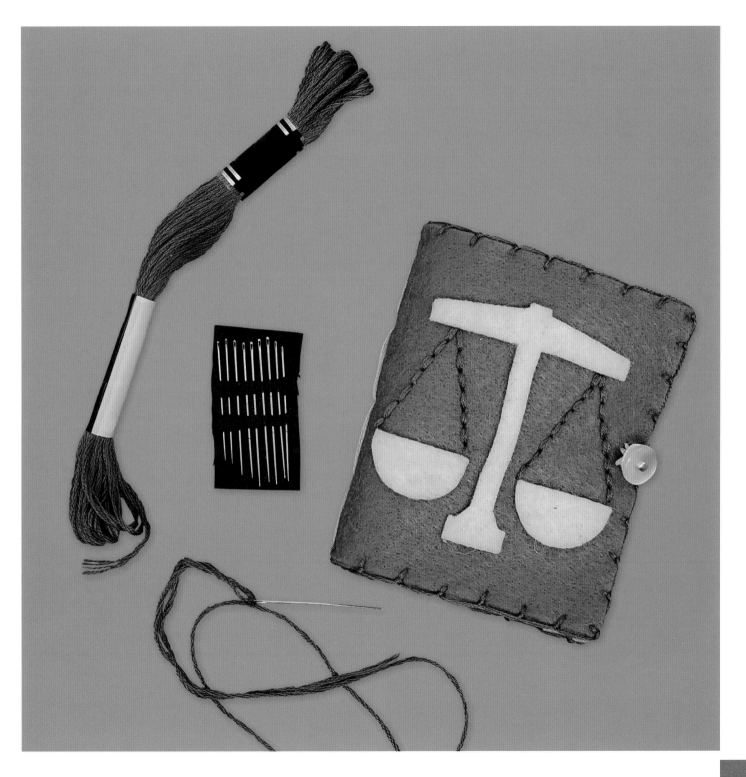

ADDING DETAILS

4 Add the stitch details as marked on the paper patterns. Use 6 strands of dark gray embroidery floss and a backstitch for the following:

- The lines for the scales on the outer cover

- The lines on the needle pockets

5 Cut out the detail pieces and remove the paper patterns. Using the pattern as a guide, hot-glue the justice scale pieces onto the front cover.

6 Using the pattern as a guide, snip a small hole in the outer cover for the elastic closure. Make a loop using the 3-inch (7.6 cm) length of elastic and glue the ends on the inside of the cover piece **(B)**.

FINISHING

7 Sew a button to the side edge of the front cover, aligning it with the loop of elastic.

8 Using the paper pattern as a guide and 6 strands of embroidery floss, assemble the cover lining as follows:

- Position the gray needle strip and use a running stitch in golden yellow to sew it in place along the side and bottom edges.

- Position the gray needle pocket and use a backstitch in golden yellow to sew it in place along the side and bottom edges.

9 Use a blanket stitch and gray embroidery floss to join the outer layer and cover lining with wrong sides together.

10 Using the paper pattern as a guide and 6 strands of embroidery floss, assemble the inner pages as follows:

- Position the gray needle pocket and use a running stitch in dark gray to sew it in place along the side and bottom edges.

- Use a backstitch in dark gray along the stitching lines to make the needle pouches in the pocket.

- Cut two slits in one of the pages at the points marked on the template and insert the 2-inch (5.1 cm) length of elastic between them **(C)**. Glue the ends of the elastic to the back of the felt page.

11 Using the paper pattern as a guide and 6 strands of embroidery floss, assemble the outer pages as follows:

- Position the gray needle pocket and use a running stitch in golden yellow to sew it in place.

- Use a backstitch in dark gray to work the lines of stitching to make the needle pouches in the pocket.

- Glue the ends of the yellow holding strips to the page. Do not attach the middle of each strip.

12 Use a blanket stitch and 6 strands of dark gray embroidery floss to join the edges of the outer and inner pages with wrong sides together.

13 Place the cover with the lining facing you. Place the pages on top with the inner pages facing you, making sure the edges are aligned. Following the dotted line on the templates, use a saddle stitch and 6 strands of golden yellow embroidery floss to stitch the pages together **(D)**.

The completed needlecase has space for your needles and embroidery floss.

PATTERN PIECES

Patterns shown at 50 percent.
Photocopy at 200 percent to enlarge
them to full size.

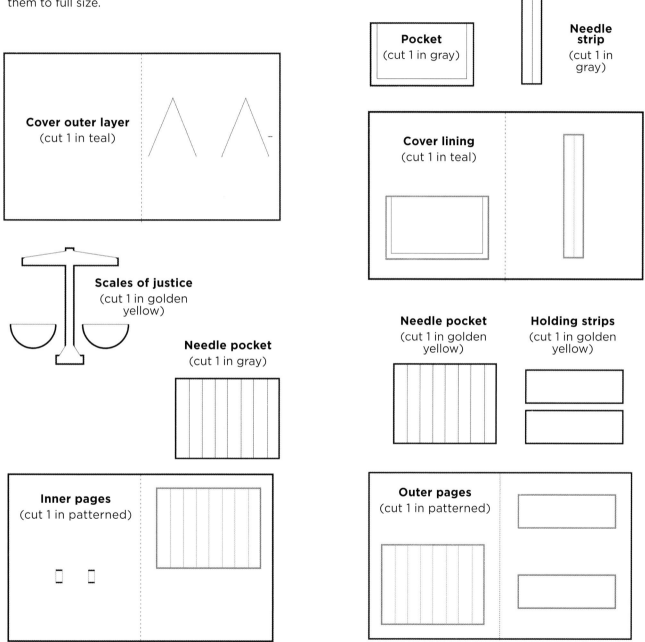

Cover outer layer
(cut 1 in teal)

Scales of justice
(cut 1 in golden
yellow)

Needle pocket
(cut 1 in gray)

Inner pages
(cut 1 in patterned)

Pocket
(cut 1 in gray)

Needle strip
(cut 1 in
gray)

Cover lining
(cut 1 in teal)

Needle pocket
(cut 1 in golden
yellow)

Holding strips
(cut 1 in golden
yellow)

Outer pages
(cut 1 in patterned)

PROTEST COASTERS

After a busy day smashing glass ceilings or fighting the patriarchy, bring the revolution home with a set of coasters. Raise a fist and a glass without scratching your coffee table!

YOU WILL NEED

1 piece of light gray felt, 4½" x 35" (11.4 x 88.9 cm)
1 piece of dark gray felt, 30" x 10" (76.2 x 25.4 cm)
1 piece of medium pink felt, 1" x 9" (2.5 x 22.9 cm)
1 piece of black felt, 6½" x 11" (16.5 x 27.9 cm)
1 piece of white felt, 7" x 4½" (17.8 x 11.4 cm)
Embroidery floss: black, dark gray, light gray, medium gray, and white

TOOLS

Paper scissors
Sticky tape
Sewing scissors
Embroidery needles
Hot glue gun and hot glue sticks
Tweezers

STITCHES

Backstitch (page 21)
Overcast stitch (page 23)

DIFFICULTY LEVEL

Easy

FINISHED SIZE

4¼" (10.8 cm) in diameter

GETTING STARTED

1 Photocopy the pattern pieces on pages 62–63 and cut them out.

2 Tape the paper pattern pieces to the felt, but avoid taping over any stitch detail marks:

- For the Raised Fist, place the base circle on light gray felt, the fist and circle outline on dark gray felt, and the fingernails on medium pink felt.

- For the Punch of Justice, place the base circle on dark gray felt, two fist pieces and circle outline on light gray felt, and the fingernail on medium pink felt.

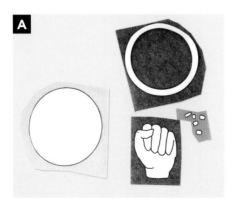

- For the Ovary Gang, place the base circle on light gray felt, two fist pieces on dark gray felt, the circle outline on black felt, and the fingernails on medium pink felt.

- For In This Together, place the base circle on black felt, two middle fist pieces and the circle outline on dark gray felt, two left fist pieces on light gray felt, two right fist pieces on white felt, and the fingernails on medium pink felt.

- For Carry the Torch, place the base circle on white felt, the hand pieces on light gray felt, the torch pieces and circle outline piece on dark gray felt, the flame pieces on black felt, and the fingernails on medium pink felt.

- For Force for Good, place the base circle piece on dark gray felt, the hand pieces and circle outline on light gray felt, and the fingernails on medium pink felt.

3 Cut out the felt pieces that do not have any marked stitch details. Keep the paper patterns to use as a guide when assembling the felt pieces.

PATTERN PIECES

Patterns shown at 40 percent.
Photocopy at 250 percent to enlarge
them to full size.

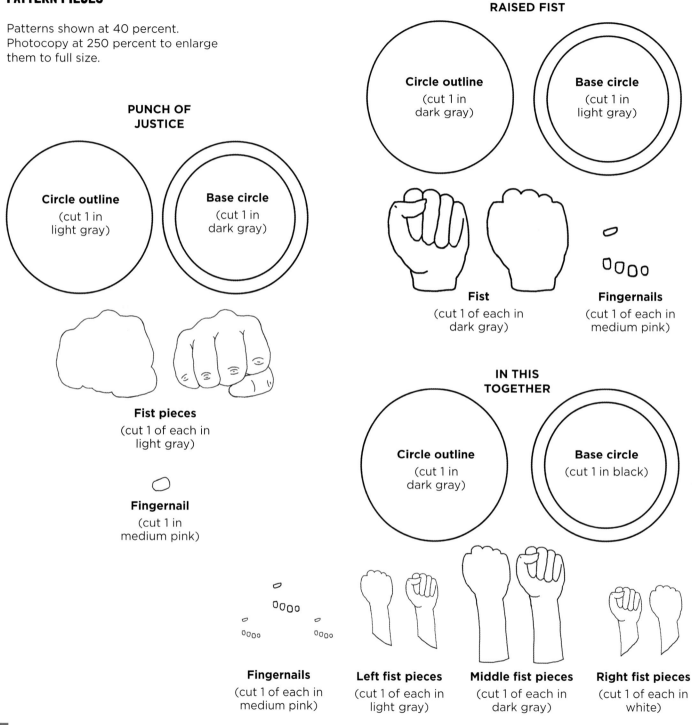

RAISED FIST

Circle outline
(cut 1 in
dark gray)

Base circle
(cut 1 in
light gray)

Fist
(cut 1 of each in
dark gray)

Fingernails
(cut 1 of each in
medium pink)

**PUNCH OF
JUSTICE**

Circle outline
(cut 1 in
light gray)

Base circle
(cut 1 in
dark gray)

Fist pieces
(cut 1 of each in
light gray)

Fingernail
(cut 1 in
medium pink)

**IN THIS
TOGETHER**

Circle outline
(cut 1 in
dark gray)

Base circle
(cut 1 in black)

Fingernails
(cut 1 of each in
medium pink)

Left fist pieces
(cut 1 of each in
light gray)

Middle fist pieces
(cut 1 of each in
dark gray)

Right fist pieces
(cut 1 of each in
white)

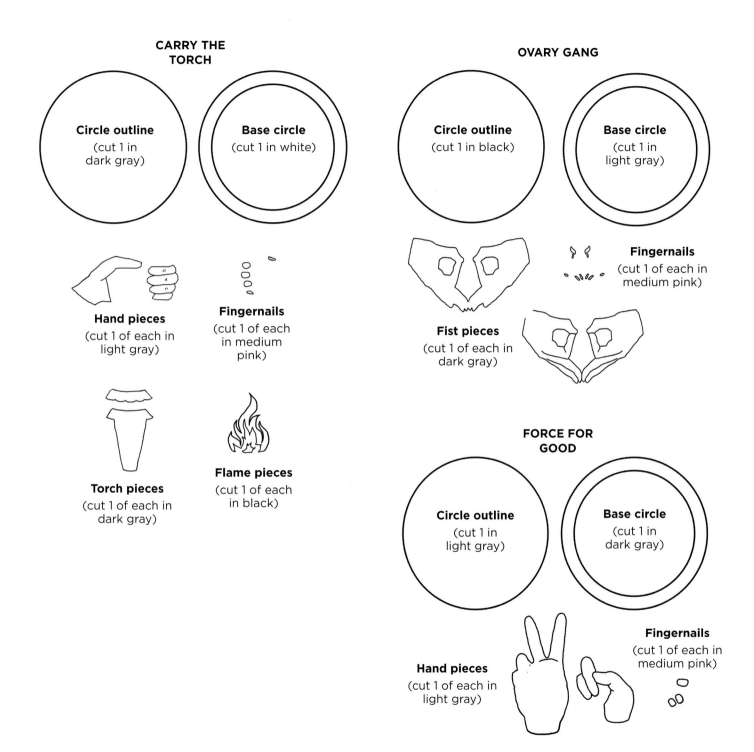

CARRY THE TORCH

Circle outline
(cut 1 in dark gray)

Base circle
(cut 1 in white)

Hand pieces
(cut 1 of each in light gray)

Fingernails
(cut 1 of each in medium pink)

Torch pieces
(cut 1 of each in dark gray)

Flame pieces
(cut 1 of each in black)

OVARY GANG

Circle outline
(cut 1 in black)

Base circle
(cut 1 in light gray)

Fingernails
(cut 1 of each in medium pink)

Fist pieces
(cut 1 of each in dark gray)

FORCE FOR GOOD

Circle outline
(cut 1 in light gray)

Base circle
(cut 1 in dark gray)

Hand pieces
(cut 1 of each in light gray)

Fingernails
(cut 1 of each in medium pink)

RIGHT TO WRITE PENCIL CASE

If the pen is mightier than the sword, you'll need a scabbard for your weapons. Carry your pens and pencils with you and be ready to capture your ideas, contribute, and make fierce art.

YOU WILL NEED

1 piece of patterned felt, 9½″ x 12″
(24.1 x 30.5 cm)

1 piece of dark purple felt, 3½″ x 7″
(8.9 x 17.8 cm)

1 piece of light purple felt, 3½″ x 7″
(8.9 x 17.8 cm)

Embroidery floss: black and dark purple

1 snap fastener

TOOLS

Paper scissors

Sticky tape

Sewing scissors

Embroidery needles

Fabric pen

Hot glue gun and hot glue sticks

Tweezers

STITCHES

Backstitch (page 21)

Running stitch (page 21)

DIFFICULTY LEVEL

Easy

FINISHED SIZE

3½″ x 8¼″ (8.9 x 21 cm)

GETTING STARTED

1 Photocopy the pattern pieces on page 67 and cut them out.

2 Tape the paper pattern pieces to the felt, but avoid taping over any stitch detail marks **(A)**:

- The case front and back pieces on patterned felt

- The Venus symbol background on dark purple felt

- The Venus symbol on light purple felt

3 Cut out the felt pieces that do not have any marked stitch details. Save a small, square scrap of patterned felt to attach the snap fastener in step 9.

ADDING DETAILS

4 Add the stitch details marked on the paper patterns. Use a running stitch and 6 strands of dark purple embroidery floss to stitch the detail around the Venus symbol and the pieces of the fist.

5 Cut out the detail pieces and remove the paper patterns. You can use hot glue to secure the loose thread ends to the back of the felt so that they don't pull through the fabric when you remove the paper.

6 To assemble the Venus symbol, hot-glue the light purple symbol onto the dark purple symbol background **(B)**.

FINISHING

7 To assemble the pencil case, align the sides of the pencil case pieces with the right sides together and use a fabric pen to mark the stitching lines along the sides and base **(C)**. Use a backstitch and black embroidery floss to stitch along the marked lines. Turn the pencil case right sides out.

8 Using the pattern as a guide, stitch the post of the snap onto the right side of the front of the case.

9 Stitch the socket of the snap onto the scrap of patterned felt. Assemble the snap. Apply hot glue to the back of the felt scrap, then fold over the flap to glue the scrap in position **(D)**.

10 Glue the Venus symbol to the front of the case.

TIP

You may find it helpful to use the fabric pen to mark the position of the snap on the felt before you sew it into position on the case.

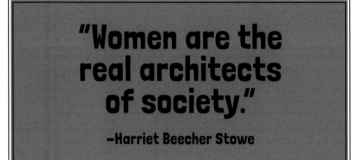

"Women are the real architects of society."

–Harriet Beecher Stowe

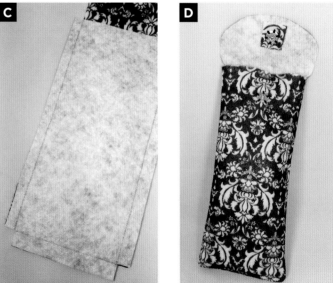

PATTERN PIECES

Patterns shown at 50 percent.
Photocopy at 200 percent to enlarge
them to full size.

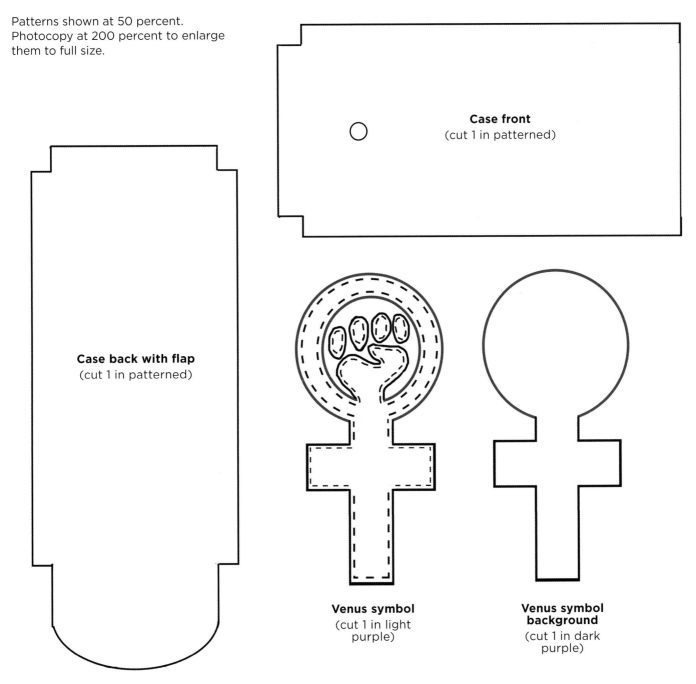

Case front
(cut 1 in patterned)

Case back with flap
(cut 1 in patterned)

Venus symbol
(cut 1 in light
purple)

**Venus symbol
background**
(cut 1 in dark
purple)

SUFFRAGETTE PURSE

The design of this purse is based on the Holloway Prison Brooch, awarded to suffragettes who had been imprisoned in the fight for the right to vote. Carry it with a strap or hold it as a clutch.

YOU WILL NEED

1 piece of dark gray felt, 18″ x 30″ (45.7 x 76.2 cm)

1 piece of light gray felt, 9″ x 15″ (22.9 x 38.1 cm)

1 piece of green felt, 1½″ x 3″ (3.8 x 7.6 cm)

1 piece of white felt, 1½″ x 3″ (3.8 x 7.6 cm)

1 piece of purple felt, 1½″ x 3″ (3.8 x 7.6 cm)

1 piece of lightweight iron-on interfacing, 18″ x 30″ (45.7 x 76.2 cm) (optional)

Embroidery floss: light gray and dark gray

1 magnetic closure

Ready-made purse strap

TOOLS

Paper scissors

Sticky tape

Sewing scissors

Embroidery needles

Hot glue gun and hot glue sticks

STITCHES

Running Stitch (page 21)

Overcast stitch (page 23)

DIFFICULTY LEVEL

Intermediate

FINISHED SIZE

6″ x 9″ x 3″ (15.2 x 22.9 x 7.6 cm)

GETTING STARTED

1 Photocopy the pattern pieces on pages 72–73 and cut them out. Because of the large size of the patterns, you'll need to tape the sections together. The dotted-line sections of the body and flap pieces should overlap **(A)**.

2 Tape the paper pattern pieces to the felt, but avoid taping over any stitch detail marks **(B)**:

- The purse inner and outer pieces, two clasp pieces, four purse sides, and four strap loop pieces on dark gray felt

- The grid pattern on light gray felt

- The clasp decoration pieces on green, white, and purple felt

3 Cut out the felt pieces.

4 If you would like to strengthen the purse, cut out a second purse inner section from the interfacing. Iron the interfacing to the inside of the inner purse felt layer according to the manufacturer's instructions (see page 14).

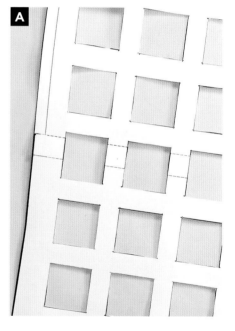

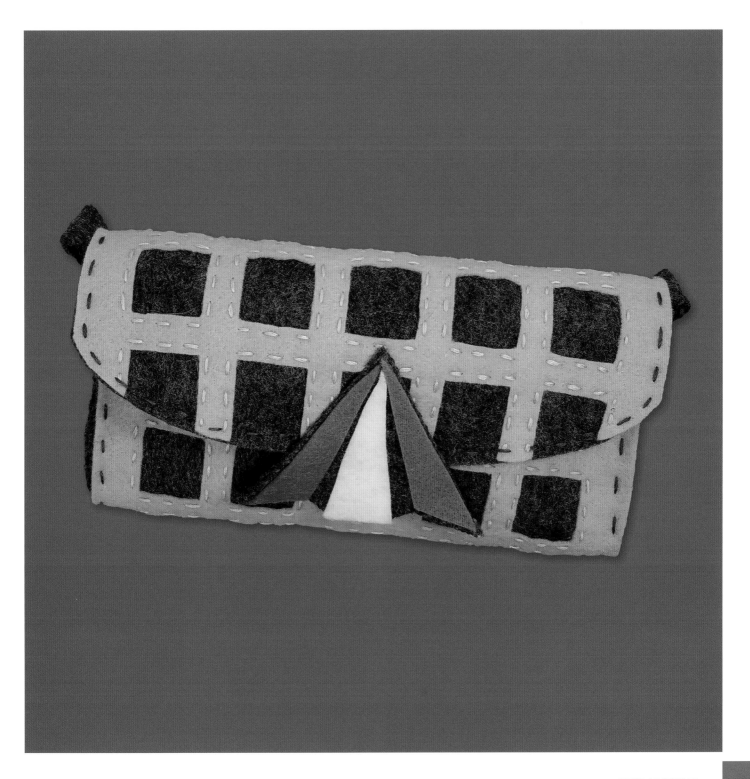

ASSEMBLING THE PURSE

5 Use hot glue to attach the grid to the outside layer of the purse, keeping the glue away from the edges of each square in the grid so you do not have to stitch through it.

6 Use a running stitch and 6 strands of light gray embroidery floss to stitch around the outline of the grid. Aim to work three stitches along each side of every grid square **(C)**.

7 Place the outer purse layer and inner purse layer together (with the interfacing on the inside, if you are using it). The dotted-line sections should line up. Apply a small dot of glue in the center of each piece to hold them in place.

8 Hold two of the side pieces together and position them against one long edge of the outer purse. Align the short, straight edges of the side pieces with the short, straight edge of the outer purse. Curve the edge of the outer piece around the edge of the side piece to create the body of the bag. Use a running stitch and 6 strands of dark gray embroidery floss to join the side and outer sections together, starting at the front of the purse and working toward the back **(D)**. Repeat for the other side of the purse.

9 After sewing the side pieces, continue to work a running stitch along the perimeter of the purse. Do not stitch along the edge of the purse's front—you will attach the magnetic closure here before sewing it closed **(E)**.

FINISHING

10 To assemble the clasp, punch the magnetic closure through one of the clasp pieces, or use the tip of a pair of scissors to make the holes in the felt. Attach the closure according to the manufacturer's instructions **(F)**.

Feminist Facts

The National Union of Women's Suffrage Societies and other suffrage groups urged their supporters to "show their colors" by wearing ribbons, buttons, and sashes in these colors. Some groups used the color green for hope, white for purity, and violet for loyalty to their cause. The first letters of these colors also echo the demand of the suffragists: Give Women the Vote. Others used white, violet, and gold, which represented light and a torch to guide the movement.

11 Stitch the two clasp layers together using 6 strands of dark gray embroidery floss and an overcast stitch. The back of the closure should be in between the two felt pieces. Place the clasp piece (magnetic closure down) on the front of the purse flap. Position the clasp as desired. Glue to the flap.

12 Close the flap. Using the clasp piece on the flap as a guide, position the other half of the magnet closure on the bottom part of the purse. Use the clasp or the tip of a pair of scissors to puncture the outer layer of the felt and insert the magnet closure **(G)**. Attach the closure according to the manufacturer's instructions.

13 Sew along the front of the purse using a running stitch and 6 strands of dark gray embroidery floss **(H)**.

14 Use hot glue to attach the green, white, and purple decoration to the clasp **(I)**.

15 Sew together the strap loops in two pairs using 6 strands of dark gray embroidery floss and an overcast stitch.

16 Fold each strap loop over one side of the purse and sew the edges together using an overcast stitch and 6 strands of dark gray embroidery floss **(J)**.

17 Add a strap to wear your purse on your shoulder, or carry it as a clutch.

TIP

Purse straps are available from fabric and craft stores and come in a variety of different materials and closures: nylon straps with hook-and-loop closures, leather straps with clips, and so on. Select a strap of your desired length and material. Follow the package instructions to attach your chosen strap. You can also repurpose a strap from an old or thrifted purse.

> "Human rights are women's rights, and women's rights are human rights."
>
> **–Hillary Clinton**

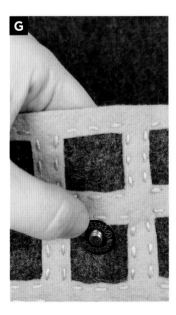

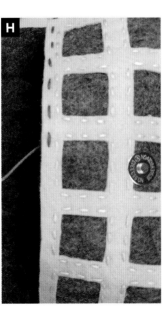

PATTERN PIECES

Patterns shown at 40 percent.
Photocopy at 250 percent to enlarge
them to full size.

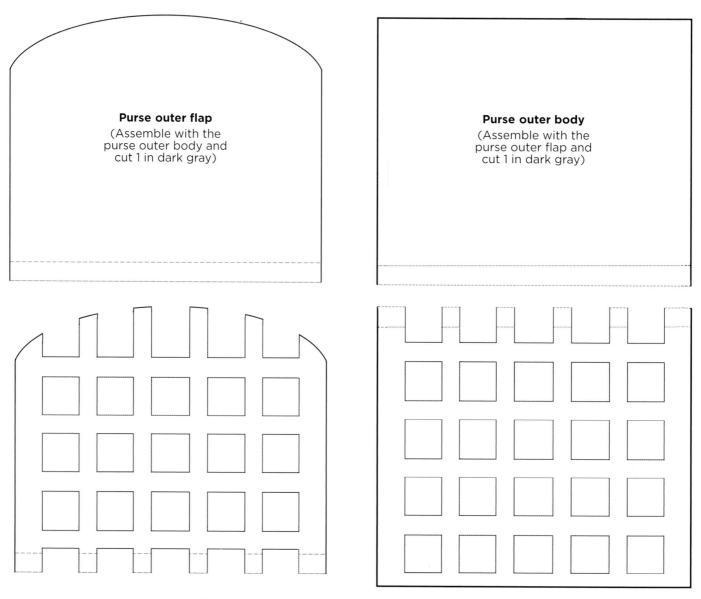

Purse outer flap
(Assemble with the
purse outer body and
cut 1 in dark gray)

Purse outer body
(Assemble with the
purse outer flap and
cut 1 in dark gray)

Grid pattern flap
(Assemble with the grid pattern
body section and cut 1 in light gray)

Grid pattern body
(Assemble with the grid pattern
flap section and cut 1 in light gray)

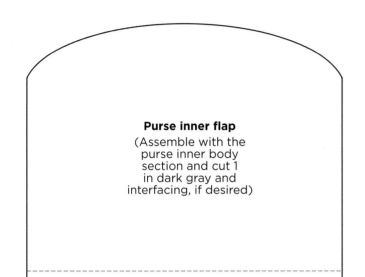

Purse inner flap
(Assemble with the
purse inner body
section and cut 1
in dark gray and
interfacing, if desired)

Purse inner body
(Assemble with the
purse inner flap
section and cut 1
in dark gray and
interfacing, if desired)

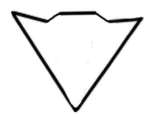

Clasp pieces
(cut 2 in
dark gray)

Clasp decoration
(cut 1 in green, white,
and purple)

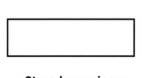

Strap loop pieces
(cut 4 in dark gray)

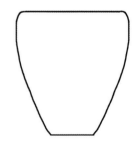

Purse sides
(cut 4 in dark gray)

CHAPTER 4

IT'S MY BODY

The very act of showing or referencing a woman's body—whether it's a diagram of a uterus in a classroom, an image of a goddess unclothed and glorious, or the representation of bodies in all its many forms—can be a radical statement. The projects in this chapter celebrate the female body. From a phone case and candleholder to a playful set of revolution-ready dress-up dolls and a scented sachet with a burning bra motif, you'll find validation and affirmation on every page.

#METOO KEY CHAIN

#MeToo is more than just a hashtag: It speaks truth to power and shows solidarity with others. This design is on a key chain because it's meant to be visible. It says: We're in this together.

YOU WILL NEED

1 piece of dark gray felt, 7" x 3" (17.8 x 7.6 cm)
1 piece of light gray felt, 7" x 3" (17.8 x 7.6 cm)
Embroidery floss: pink and dark gray
One ⅛-inch (5 mm) grommet
1 key ring

TOOLS

Paper scissors
Sticky tape
Sewing scissors
Embroidery needles
Hot glue gun and hot glue sticks
Grommet kit and hammer

STITCHES

Backstitch (page 21)
Overcast stitch (page 23)

DIFFICULTY LEVEL

Easy

FINISHED SIZE

3⅛" x 2½" (8 x 6.4 cm)

GETTING STARTED

1 Photocopy the pattern pieces on page 79 and cut them out.

2 Tape the paper pattern pieces to the felt, but avoid taping over any stitch detail marks **(A)**:

- The front and back pieces on dark gray felt
- The filling and lettering on light gray felt

3 Cut out the felt pieces that do not have any marked stitch details.

ADDING DETAILS

4 Add the stitch details as marked on the paper patterns using a backstitch and 6 strands of pink embroidery floss **(B)**.

5 Cut out the detail pieces and remove the paper patterns. You can use hot glue to secure the loose thread ends to the back of the felt so that they don't pull through the fabric when you remove the paper.

FINISHING

6 To assemble the key chain base, glue the filling piece on top of the back piece **(C)**, then glue the front piece on top of the filling.

7 Use an overcast stitch and 6 strands of dark gray embroidery floss to stitch around the edges of the key chain **(D)**.

8 Position the lettering on the top of the key chain, then glue in place.

9 Following the package instructions, use the grommet kit to affix the grommets and reinforce the hole at the center of the hashtag. Attach the key ring to the key chain using the grommet.

> **"My courage always rises with every attempt to intimidate me."**
>
> –Jane Austen, *Pride and Prejudice*

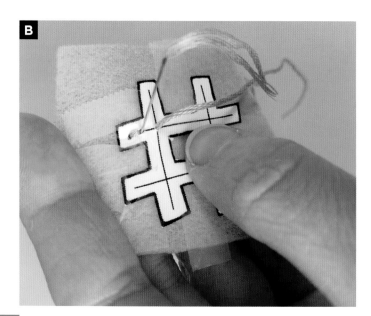

PATTERN PIECES

Patterns shown true to size.
Photocopy at 100 percent.

Lettering
(cut 1 in
light gray)

Filling
(cut 1 in
light gray)

Back piece
(cut 1 in
dark gray)

Front piece
(cut 1 in
dark gray)

THE SMELL OF REVOLUTION

Nothing is sweeter than the smell of revolution. Fill this sachet with potpourri, or dab the fabric filling with your favorite essential oil, and dream of a revolutionary future.

YOU WILL NEED

1 piece of black felt, 6½" x 10" (16.5 x 25.4 cm)
1 piece of red felt, 5" x 8" (12.7 x 20.3 cm)
1 piece of orange felt, 3½" x 6" (8.9 x 15.2 cm)
1 piece of yellow felt, 2" x 2½" (5.1 x 6.4 cm)
1 piece of pink felt, 3" x 7" (7.6 x 17.8 cm)
Embroidery floss: black, pink, and orange
Cotton fabric scraps
Essential oils or loose potpourri

TOOLS

Paper scissors
Sticky tape
Sewing scissors
Embroidery needles
Hot glue gun and hot glue sticks

STITCHES

Backstitch (page 21)
Overcast stitch (page 23)

DIFFICULTY LEVEL

Easy

FINISHED SIZE

4" x 6" (10.2 x 15.2 cm)

GETTING STARTED

1 Photocopy the pattern pieces on page 83 and cut them out.

2 Tape the paper pattern pieces to the felt, but avoid taping over any stitch detail marks **(A)**:

- The background pieces on black felt

- The large flames on red felt
- The medium flames on orange felt
- The small flames on yellow felt
- The bra pieces on pink

3 Cut out all the felt pieces, except the ones for the bra.

A

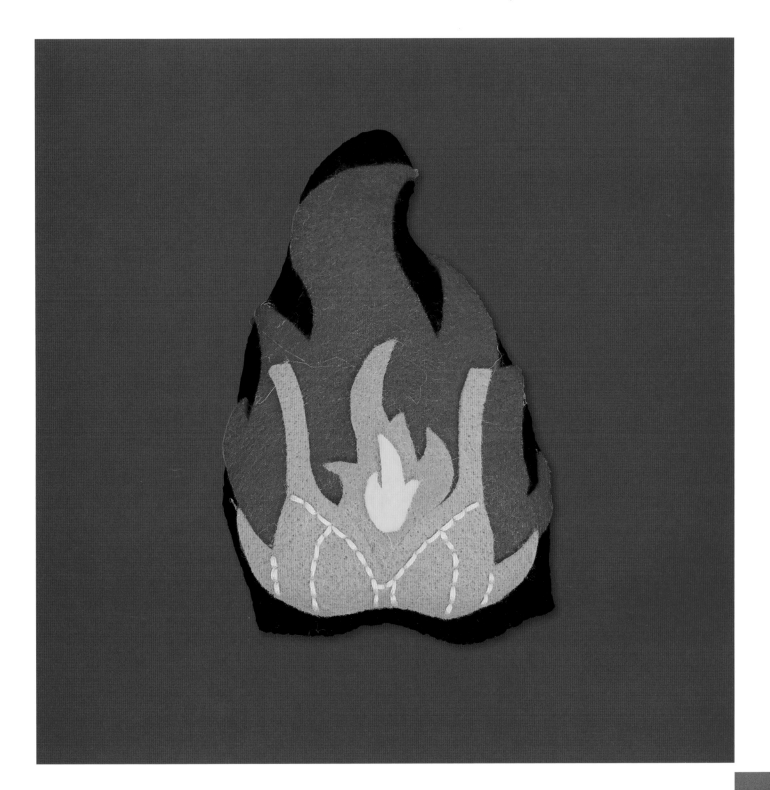

ADDING DETAILS

4 Use a backstitch and 6 strands of pink embroidery floss to stitch the details on the front and back bra pieces.

5 Cut out the bra pieces and remove the paper patterns. You can use hot glue to secure the loose thread ends to the back of the felt so that they don't pull through the fabric when you remove the paper.

6 Position the front and back orange flames on the corresponding red flames and join the pieces together using the overcast stitch and 6 strands of orange embroidery floss. Do not sew the top—this will be the pocket that holds the potpourri or scented fabric.

7 Use hot glue to attach the red front and back flames to their respective black backgrounds **(B)**.

FINISHING

8 Place the background layers with right sides together. Use a backstitch and 6 strands of black embroidery floss to sew around the perimeter of the sachet, about ¼ inch (5 mm) from the edge. Be sure to leave a generous hole at the bottom for turning your sachet right side out.

9 Turn the sachet right side out, making sure the corners have been poked out and are smooth.

10 If using cotton fabric scraps, sprinkle them with a few drops of essential oil.

11 Fill the sachet with potpourri or the scented fabric. Use an overcast stitch and 6 strands of black embroidery floss to close the hole **(C)**.

10 Use hot glue to attach the back bra piece to the back of the sachet, taking care not to glue the pocket shut. Glue the yellow flames to the back of the sachet.

11 Use hot glue to attach the front bra piece to the front of the sachet. Glue the orange and yellow flames in place on top of the larger flames, above the bra **(D)**.

TIP

Cotton fabric scraps are the best choice for filling as they will absorb the essential oils better than polyester fiberfill or acrylic felt.

Feminist Facts

The legend that feminists burned their bras began after a protest against the 1968 Miss America pageant. The demonstration aimed to challenge attitudes towards women and the "ludicrous 'beauty' standards" imposed on them. Protesters were encouraged to throw items that symbolized male-dominated culture into a Freedom Trash Can. The can was filled with high heels, copies of *Playboy* magazine, makeup, girdles, and bras. A rumor that the trash can was then set on fire was just that, but it created the myth of bra-burning feminists. The protest did little to change the pageant, but it introduced feminism to a wider audience.

PATTERN PIECES

Patterns shown at 40 percent.
Photocopy at 250 percent to
enlarge them to full size.

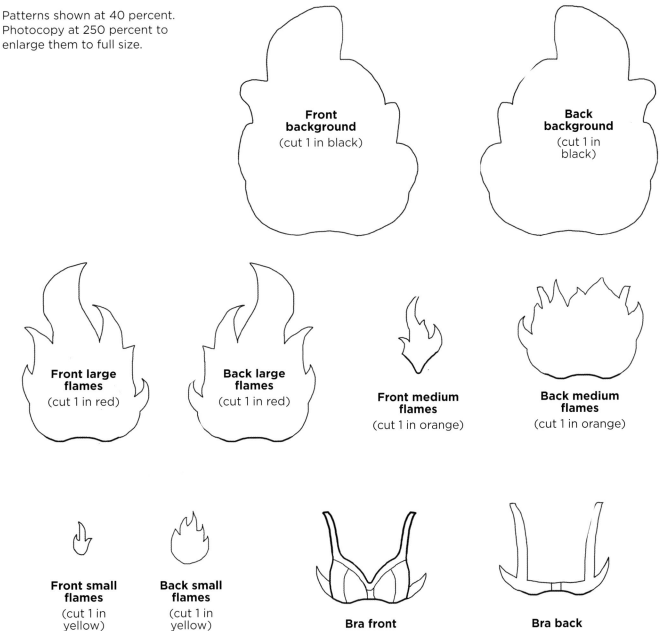

Front
background
(cut 1 in black)

Back
background
(cut 1 in
black)

Front large
flames
(cut 1 in red)

Back large
flames
(cut 1 in red)

Front medium
flames
(cut 1 in orange)

Back medium
flames
(cut 1 in orange)

Front small
flames
(cut 1 in
yellow)

Back small
flames
(cut 1 in
yellow)

Bra front
(cut 1 in pink)

Bra back
(cut 1 in pink)

GAIA GODDESS PHONE CASE

Elevate your smartphone with the image of Gaia, goddess of Earth. This ancient image of strength and womanhood flexes her muscles, as you stretch your networking abilities with your phone.

YOU WILL NEED

1 piece of dark gray felt, 11¼" x 14" (28.6 x 35.6 cm)

1 piece of green patterned felt, 4" x 9" (10.2 x 22.9 cm)

Embroidery floss: dark gray and green

Note: Adjust measurements to fit your phone.

TOOLS

Paper scissors

Sticky tape

Sewing scissors

Embroidery needles

Hot glue gun and hot glue sticks

STITCHES

Running stitch (page 21)

DIFFICULTY LEVEL

Easy

FINISHED SIZE

3½" x 10" (8.9 x 25.4 cm)

GETTING STARTED

1 Photocopy the pattern pieces on page 87 and cut them out.

2 Tape the paper pattern pieces to the felt, but avoid taping over any stitch detail marks **(A)**:

- The phone case pieces on dark gray felt
- The Gaia and strap pieces on the patterned green felt

3 Cut out all the felt pieces.

The great Greek Earth mother!

ASSEMBLING THE CASE

4 Place the strap pieces with right sides together. Use a running stitch and 6 strands of dark gray embroidery floss to stitch the strap pieces together on the long edges.

5 Place all the pieces for the front and back of the case together so they are aligned at the sides and bottom. Position the strap on the back of the case. It will hold the flap in place so check that it will do so securely **(B)**.

6 Use 6 strands of green embroidery floss and a running stitch to sew all the layers together **(C)**. Stitch around the edge of the case. Do not stitch the opening of the case closed.

FINISHING

7 Fold the flap into place. Position the Gaia figure on the front of the phone case **(D)**. When you are satisfied with the placement, use hot glue to attach it to the case, one piece at a time, starting with the head and body and finishing with the arms.

> # "Gaia, mother of all, eldest of all beings."
>
> **–Homeric Hymn XXX to Gaia**

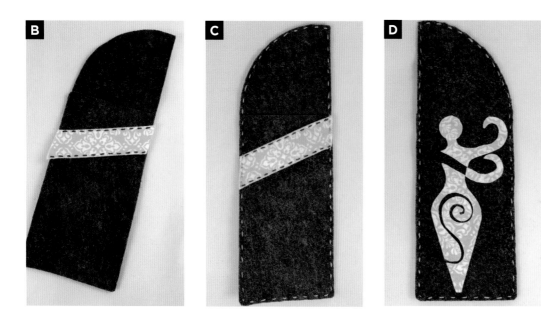

B

C

D

Feminist Facts

Gaia, the Greek goddess of the Earth, was the mother of all the other Greek gods. Today, some earth scientists use the term *Gaia* to describe a theory known as the Gaia hypothesis, the idea that the Earth is a complex and complete living planet.

PATTERN PIECES

Patterns shown at 60 percent.
Photocopy at 167 percent to enlarge
them to full size.

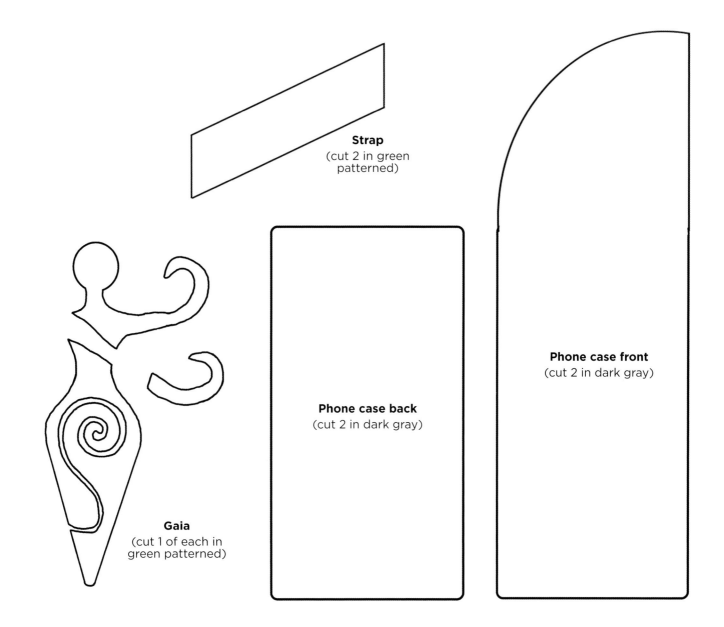

Strap
(cut 2 in green
patterned)

Phone case front
(cut 2 in dark gray)

Phone case back
(cut 2 in dark gray)

Gaia
(cut 1 of each in
green patterned)

FIERY FEMALES CANDLEHOLDER

This circle of women celebrates the beauty of our diversity. Place a glass with a tea light in the center of this circle of power, and make our beauty shine in its many shapes and colors!

YOU WILL NEED

1 piece of cream felt, 3½" x 4½" (8.9 x 11.4 cm)

1 piece of beige felt, 3½" x 4½" (8.9 x 11.4 cm)

1 piece of light tan felt, 3½" x 4½" (8.9 x 11.4 cm)

1 piece of light brown felt, 3½" x 4½" (8.9 x 11.4 cm)

1 piece of medium brown felt, 3½" x 4½" (8.9 x 11.4 cm)

1 piece of dark brown felt, 3½" x 4½" (8.9 x 11.4 cm)

1 piece of black felt, 14" x 20" (35.6 x 50.8 cm)

Embroidery floss: cream, beige, light tan, light brown, medium brown, dark brown, and black

TOOLS

Paper scissors

Sticky tape

Sewing scissors

Embroidery needles

Hot glue gun and hot glue sticks

STITCHES

Overcast stitch (page 23)

DIFFICULTY LEVEL

Easy

FINISHED SIZE

4" x 5" (10.2 x 12.7 cm)

GETTING STARTED

1 Photocopy the pattern pieces on page 91 and cut them out. Because of the large size of the background you'll need to tape the sections together. The dotted-line sections of the body and flap pieces overlap.

2 Tape the paper pattern pieces to the felt, but avoid taping over any stitch detail marks **(A)**:

- One female figure on each color felt: cream, beige, light tan, light brown, medium brown, and dark brown

- The background figure strip, two circular bases, and the bottom strip on black felt

3 Cut out the felt pieces.

ADDING DETAILS

4 Use hot glue to join the two circular base pieces together. Only apply glue in the center of the pieces.

5 Arrange the female figures on the background figure strip. When you are happy with the placement, use a dot of glue to hold each one in place.

6 Using 6 strands of the embroidery floss that matches the color of the felt figure that you are attaching, stitch the figures onto the background using an overcast stitch **(B)**.

FINISHING

7 Attach the circular base to the bottom edge of the background figure strip using 6 strands of black embroidery floss and an overcast stitch.

8 Join the figures in a ring by hooking together the arms of the figures at each end of the background figure strip **(C)**. Use a dab of glue to keep their arms in place, if desired.

9 Glue the bottom strip around the base of the figures so that it covers their feet **(D)**.

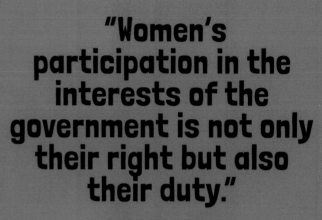

> *"Women's participation in the interests of the government is not only their right but also their duty."*
>
> **–Louise Otto–Peters**

B

C

D

PATTERN PIECES

Patterns shown at 40 percent.
Photocopy at 250 percent to enlarge
them to full size.

**Background
figure strip**
(Assemble with the
other background
figure strip section
and cut 1 in black)

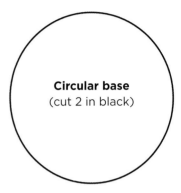

Circular base
(cut 2 in black)

Bottom strip
(Assemble with
the other bottom
strip section and
cut 1 in black)

Background figure strip
(Assemble with the other
background figure strip
section and cut 1 in black)

Figures
(cut 1 in cream,
beige, light tan,
light brown,
medium brown,
and dark brown)

Bottom strip
(Assemble with
the other bottom
strip section and
cut 1 in black)

DRESS FOR THE REVOLUTION DOLLS

Put on your pink pussy hat, don your symbol of Venus T-shirt, lace up your suffragette boots, or put on your white pantsuit, and dress this magnet doll for the revolution.

YOU WILL NEED

1 piece of skin-tone felt (medium tan, light brown, and dark brown shown), 9″ x 10″ (22.9 x 25.4 cm)

1 piece of black felt, 9″ x 14″ (22.9 x 35.6 cm)

1 piece of white felt, 7″ x 12″ (17.8 x 30.5 cm)

1 piece of blue felt, 2″ x 5″ (5.1 x 12.7 cm)

1 piece of dark brown felt, 3″ x 7″ (7.6 x 17.8 cm)

1 piece of light brown felt, 2″ x 4″ (5.1 x 10.2 cm)

1 piece of pink felt, 1″ x 4″ (2.5 x 10.2 cm)

1 piece of red felt, 2″ x 2½″ (5.1 x 6.4 cm)

1 piece of yellow felt, 2½″ x 6″ (6.4 x 15.2 cm)

1 piece of burgundy felt, 2½″ x 4″ (6.4 x 10.2 cm)

Twenty-nine ¼-inch (5 mm) round magnets

Embroidery floss: black, skin tone (medium tan, light brown, or dark brown), white, blue, dark brown, light brown, pink, and burgundy

TOOLS

Paper scissors

Sticky tape

Sewing scissors

Embroidery needles

Hot glue gun and hot glue sticks

Tweezers

STITCHES

French knot (page 25)

Backstitch (page 21)

Overcast stitch (page 23)

DIFFICULTY LEVEL

Intermediate

FINISHED SIZE

Approximately 5″ x 9″ (12.7 x 22.9 cm), varies according to the accessories used

GETTING STARTED

1 Photocopy the pattern pieces on pages 96–97 and cut them out.

2 Tape the paper pattern pieces to the felt, but avoid taping over any stitch detail marks **(A)**:

- The head and two body pieces on skin-tone felt

- The underwear piece on black felt

- For the Suffragette: one dress piece, and one dress piece without the collar and cuffs on black felt, and four boot pieces (two for each boot) on black felt

- For the Power Pantsuit: two shirt and collar pieces and two pant pieces on white felt, and four heel pieces (two for each shoe) on red felt

- For the Revolution Uniform: two T-shirt pieces on white felt, two skirt pieces on blue felt, four boot pieces (two for each boot) on dark brown felt, and two hat pieces and one hat brim on pink felt

- For the hair: two bobbed pieces on light brown felt, two flipped hair pieces on yellow felt, two wavy hair pieces on burgundy felt, two bouffant hair pieces and the bangs on black felt, and two suffragette hair pieces on dark brown felt

3 Cut out the felt pieces that do not have any marked stitch details.

A

ADDING DETAILS

3 Add the stitch details as marked on the paper patterns using the number of strands of embroidery floss listed.

For the Body, use:

- A backstitch in brown (3 strands) for the knees on the body

- French knots in black (6 strands) for the eyes on the head **(B)**

- A backstitch in red (3 strands) for the mouth on the head

- A backstitch in black (3 strands) for the nose on the head

For the Suffragette, use:

- French knots in white (6 strands) for the buttons on the upper layer of the dress **(C)**

For the Power Pantsuit, use:

- A backstitch in light gray (3 strands) for the center seam detail on the shirt

For the Revolution Uniform, use:

- A backstitch in pink (6 strands) for the Venus symbol on the T-shirt

4 Use the dots on the pattern pieces to position the magnets. Be sure to pay attention to the polarity of the magnets and check that they are all placed consistently. Glue around (not under or over) the magnets to attach them firmly **(D)**.

FINISHING

5 To assemble the body, remove the paper pattern pieces and align the body and undergarment pieces. Sew the pieces together using 6 strands of embroidery floss as follows:

- An overcast stitch in black to sew the edges of the underwear to the body, stitching through all the layers

- An overcast stitch in skin tone to sew the remaining edges of the body pieces together **(E)**

6 To assemble the Suffragette, remove the paper pattern pieces. Sew the pieces together using 6 strands of embroidery floss as follows:

- Use an overcast stitch in black to sew the two dress pieces together.

- Glue the collar piece and cuffs onto the dress. Use tweezers to hold the felt as you're gluing **(H)**.

- Use an overcast stitch in black to sew the edges of the boots together to make a pair.

> ### TIP
>
> Magnets have a north and a south pole; opposite poles attract and like poles repel. Before you attach the magnets, make sure that when the clothes are positioned on the doll, the opposite poles are aligned so that they attract rather than repel.

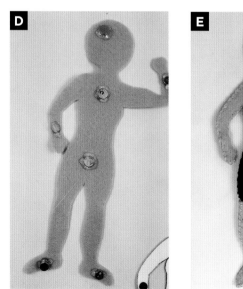

7 To assemble the Power Pantsuit, remove the paper pattern pieces from the shirt pieces. Sew the pieces together using 6 strands of embroidery floss as follows:

- Use an overcast stitch in white to sew the two shirt pieces together.

- Glue the collar pieces onto the collar of the shirt. Use tweezers to hold the felt as you're gluing **(G)**.

- Use an overcast stitch in white to sew the edges of the pant pieces together.

- Use an overcast stitch in red to sew the edges of the shoes together to make a pair.

8 To assemble the Revolution Uniform, remove the paper pattern pieces. Sew the pieces together using 6 strands of embroidery floss as follows:

- Use an overcast stitch in white to sew the edges of the shirt pieces together **(F)**.

- Use an overcast stitch in blue to sew the edges of the skirt pieces together.

- Use an overcast stitch in brown to sew the edges of the boots together to make a pair.

- Use an overcast stitch in pink to sew the edges of the hat pieces together.

- Glue the brim onto the hat piece.

9 To assemble the hair pieces remove the paper pattern pieces. Sew the pieces together using 6 strands of embroidery floss as follows:

- Use an overcast stitch in brown to sew the bobbed hair pieces together.

- Glue the two hair pieces for the flip together.

- Use an overcast stitch in burgundy to sew the edges of the wavy hair pieces together.

- Use an overcast stitch in black to sew the main bouffant hair pieces together. Glue on the bangs **(I)**.

- Glue the two hair pieces for the Suffragette hair together.

F

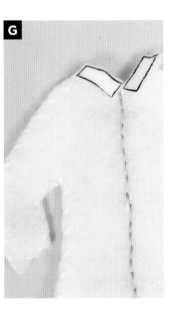

G

H

I

PATTERN PIECES

Patterns shown at 50 percent.
Photocopy at 200 percent to enlarge
them to full size.

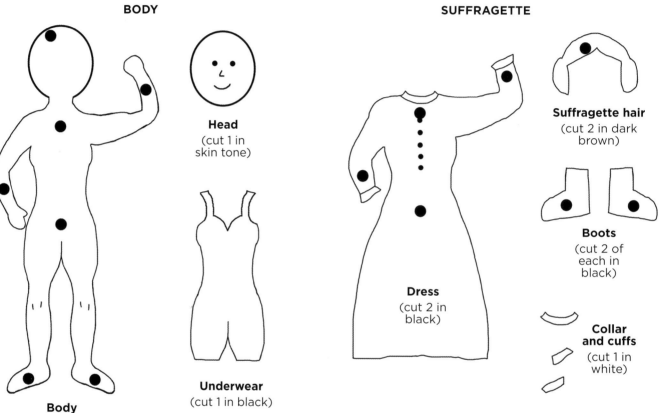

BODY

SUFFRAGETTE

Head
(cut 1 in
skin tone)

Suffragette hair
(cut 2 in dark
brown)

Boots
(cut 2 of
each in
black)

Dress
(cut 2 in
black)

**Collar
and cuffs**
(cut 1 in
white)

Underwear
(cut 1 in black)

Body
(cut 2 in
skin tone)

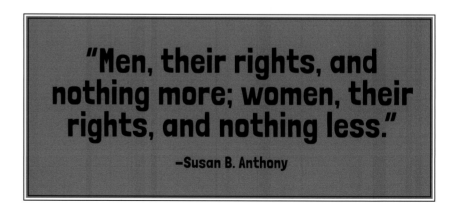

> "Men, their rights, and nothing more; women, their rights, and nothing less."
>
> –Susan B. Anthony

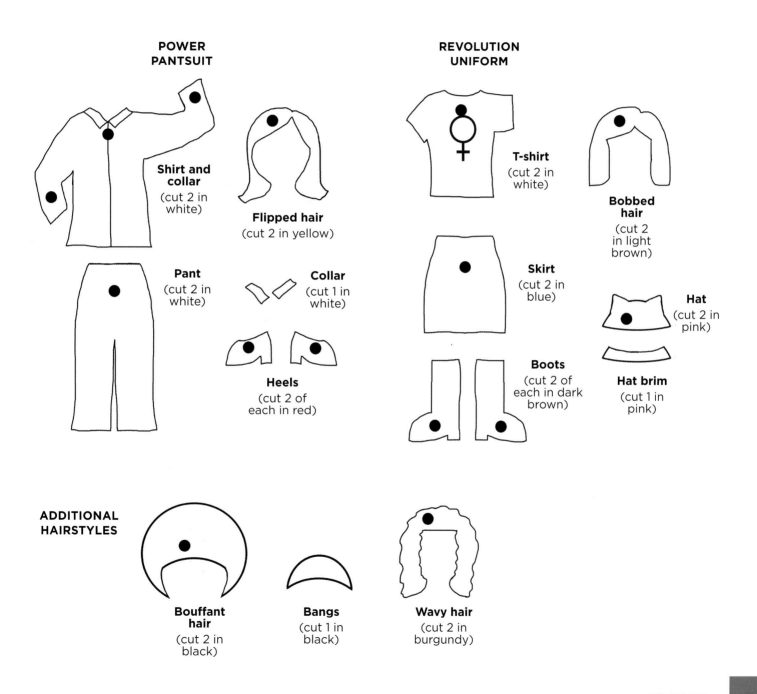

POWER PANTSUIT

Shirt and collar
(cut 2 in white)

Flipped hair
(cut 2 in yellow)

Pant
(cut 2 in white)

Collar
(cut 1 in white)

Heels
(cut 2 of each in red)

REVOLUTION UNIFORM

T-shirt
(cut 2 in white)

Bobbed hair
(cut 2 in light brown)

Skirt
(cut 2 in blue)

Boots
(cut 2 of each in dark brown)

Hat
(cut 2 in pink)

Hat brim
(cut 1 in pink)

ADDITIONAL HAIRSTYLES

Bouffant hair
(cut 2 in black)

Bangs
(cut 1 in black)

Wavy hair
(cut 2 in burgundy)

FEISTY FESTIVE ORNAMENT

The most adorable reproductive organ on your tree, the uterus (or cute-erus) is just happy to be here. Who knew that fallopian tubes could look so festive?

YOU WILL NEED

1 piece of dark pink felt, 6" x 8" (15.2 x 20.3 cm)
1 piece of light pink felt, 3" x 3½" (7.6 x 8.9 cm)
1 piece of white felt, 2" x 3" (5.1 x 7.6 cm)
1 piece of dark gray felt, 2" x 2" (5.1 x 5.1 cm)
12-inch (30.5 cm) length of ribbon (any color)
Embroidery floss: white, light pink, and dark pink

TOOLS

Paper scissors
Sticky tape
Sewing scissors
Embroidery needles
Hot glue gun and hot glue sticks
Tweezers

STITCHES

Running stitch (page 21)
Overcast stitch (page 23)

DIFFICULTY LEVEL

Easy

FINISHED SIZE

4" x 6" (10.2 x 15.2 cm)

GETTING STARTED

1 Photocopy the pattern pieces on page 101 and cut them out.

2 Tape the paper pattern pieces to the felt, but avoid taping over any stitch detail marks **(A)**:

- The background pieces on dark pink felt

- The uterine wall pieces on light pink felt

- The ovaries and pupil pieces on white felt

- The eyes, eyebrows, and mouth pieces on dark gray felt

3 Cut out the felt pieces that do not have any marked stitch details.

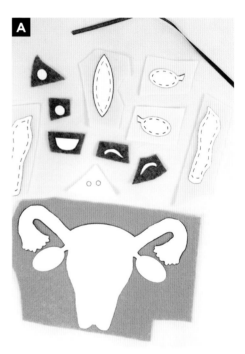

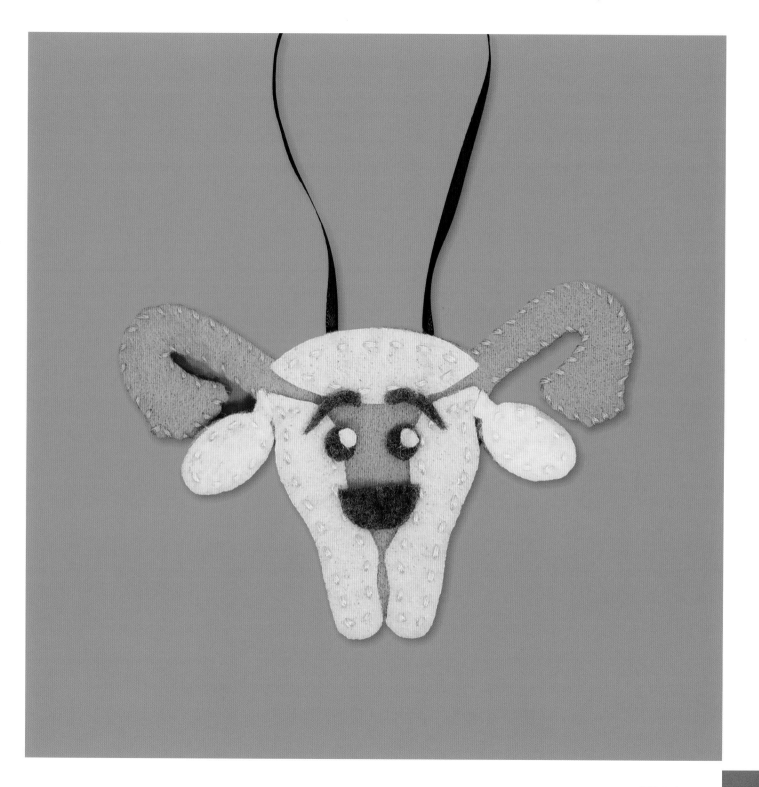

ADDING DETAILS

4 Use a running stitch and 6 strands of light pink embroidery floss to sew the detail onto the uterine wall pieces, and white embroidery floss to stitch the detail onto the ovaries.

5 Cut out the detail pieces and remove the paper patterns. You can use hot glue to secure the loose thread ends at the back of the felt so that they don't pull through the fabric when you remove the paper.

FINISHING

6 Use hot glue to join the two dark pink background pieces together. Be sure to avoid the edges as you will stitch through them later. Glue the ribbon in between the background pieces at the top of the ornament **(B)**.

7 Use the overcast stitch and 6 strands of pink embroidery floss to sew the two background pieces together **(C)**.

8 Use hot glue to join the remaining pieces together. Use tweezers to hold the felt as you're gluing the pieces as follows:

- The uterine walls and ovaries to the background
- The pupils to the eyes
- The eyes and eyebrows to the main ornament
- The mouth piece to the main ornament **(D)**

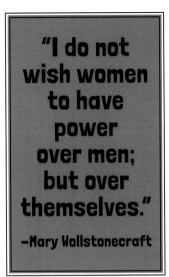

> "I do not wish women to have power over men; but over themselves."
>
> –Mary Wollstonecraft

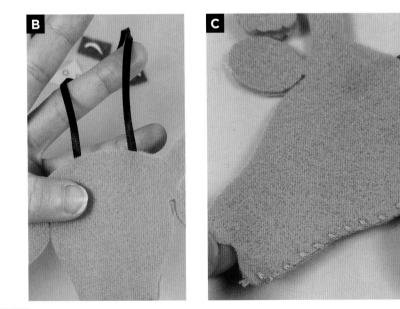

PATTERN PIECES

Patterns shown true to size. Photocopy at 100 percent.

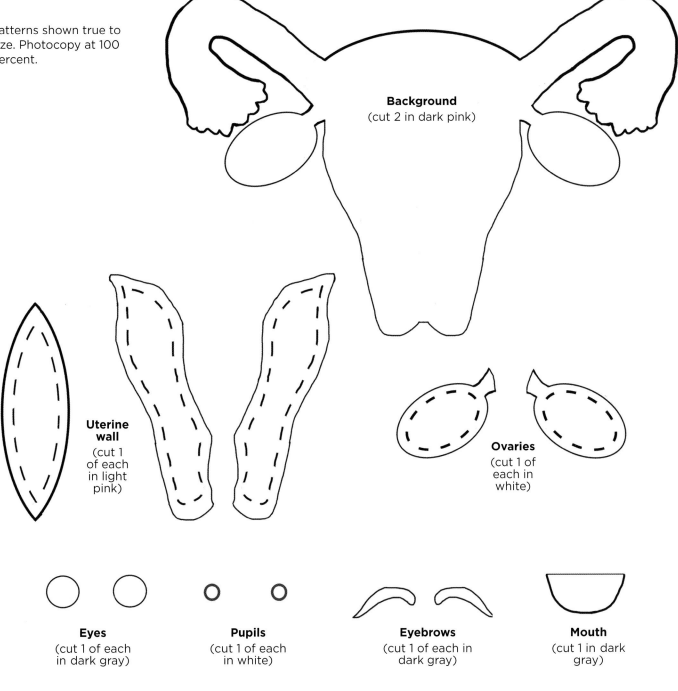

Background
(cut 2 in dark pink)

Uterine wall
(cut 1 of each in light pink)

Ovaries
(cut 1 of each in white)

Eyes
(cut 1 of each in dark gray)

Pupils
(cut 1 of each in white)

Eyebrows
(cut 1 of each in dark gray)

Mouth
(cut 1 in dark gray)

CHAPTER 5

FEMINIST FASHIONISTA

Incorporating objects with a feminist message, nod, or smile into your daily life can be a powerful reminder of empowering values—even if they aren't immediately apparent to others. Giving these objects as gifts can also be both a show of solidarity and friendship. These fabulous objects are practical and delightful, and have a feminist thread running through their design, from the yellow suffragette rose stitched into the Little Flower Tampon Roll, to the pink of the Pussycat Coffee Cozy.

VENUS FLYTRAP POT COVER

The Venus flytrap was named after the Roman goddess of love and has come to symbolize feminine cunning and ingenuity. Decorate your home with this sly nod to feminine power.

YOU WILL NEED

1 piece of light gray felt, 18" x 24" (45.7 x 61 cm)
1 piece of dark green felt, 6" x 18" (15.2 x 45.7 cm)
1 piece of light green felt, 4" x 5" (10.2 x 12.7 cm)
1 piece of light pink felt, 2" x 4" (5.1 x 10.2 cm)
1 piece of dark pink felt, 1" x 4" (2.5 x 10.2 cm)
Embroidery floss: dark green, white, and light gray

TOOLS

Embroidery needles
Sewing scissors
Paper scissors
Sticky tape
Hot glue gun and hot glue sticks
Tweezers

STITCHES

Backstitch (page 21)
Overcast stitch (page 23)

DIFFICULTY LEVEL

Easy

FINISHED SIZE

Fits a 5½-inch (14 cm) tall flowerpot
Rim diameter: 6" (15.2 cm)
Base diameter: 3½" (8.9 cm)
Height: 5¾" (14.6 cm)

GETTING STARTED

1 Photocopy the pattern pieces on page 107 and cut them out. Because of the large size of the wrap and rim patterns, you'll need to tape the pieces together. The dotted-line sections of the body and flap pieces should overlap. You may find it helpful to number the leaf and flytrap pieces to help you keep track of their order and placement.

2 Tape the paper pattern pieces to the felt, but avoid taping over any stitch detail marks **(A)**:

- The pot wrap and two base pieces on light gray felt
- The pot rim piece and some of the leaves and outer Venus flytrap pieces on dark green felt
- The remaining leaves and the outer Venus flytrap pieces on light green felt
- The middle Venus flytrap pieces on light pink felt
- The inner Venus flytrap pieces on dark pink felt

3 Cut out all the pieces except the pot wrap.

ADDING DETAILS

4 Place the middle flytrap pieces on top of the green outer pieces and use hot glue to join them at the edges. Do not glue them at the center. Repeat to attach the inner flytrap pieces on top of the middle pieces **(B)**.

5 Using the solid lines marked on the pattern for the pot wrap as a guide, stitch the leaves onto the pot using a backstitch and 6 strands of dark green embroidery floss. Do not stitch along the dotted lines as these are where the flytrap pieces will be added **(C)**.

6 Position the flytrap pieces on the pot wrap on the spaces marked by dotted lines on the pattern. Use 6 strands of white embroidery floss and a backstitch to sew the flytrap pieces onto the pot by stitching through the center of each flytrap piece **(D)**.

7 Cut out the pot wrap and carefully remove the paper pattern. You can use hot glue to secure the loose thread ends to the back of the felt so that they don't pull through the fabric when you remove the paper.

FINISHING

8 Using 6 strands of light gray embroidery floss and an overcast stitch, sew the ends of the pot wrap together.

9 Use hot glue to join the two base pieces together at their centers. Using 6 strands of light gray embroidery floss and an overcast stitch, sew the edge of the base to the bottom of the wrap piece.

10 Wrap the pot rim around the top of the pot wrap and hot-glue in place. Alternatively, it can be attached using 6 strands of light gray embroidery floss and an overcast stitch.

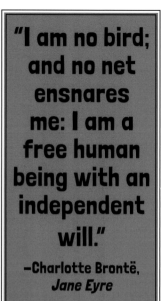

"I am no bird; and no net ensnares me: I am a free human being with an independent will."
—Charlotte Brontë, *Jane Eyre*

B

C

D

PATTERN PIECES

Patterns shown at 35 percent.
Photocopy at 286 percent to enlarge
them to full size.

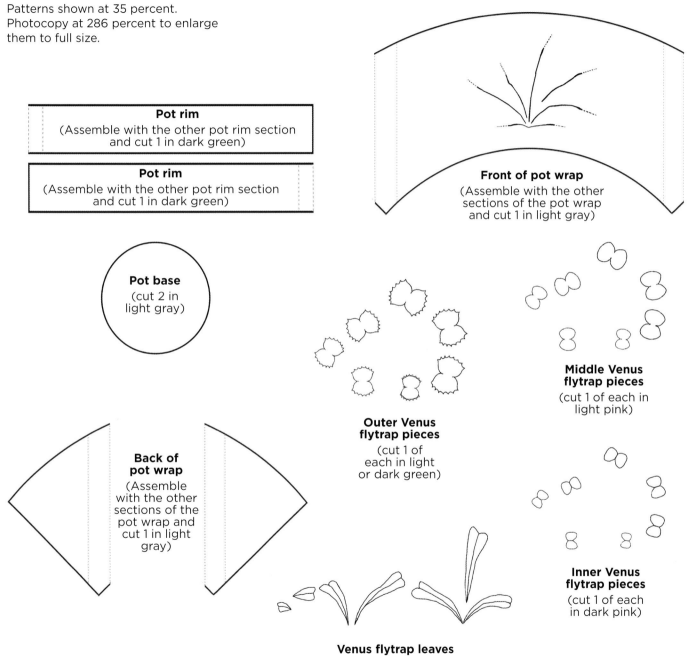

Pot rim
(Assemble with the other pot rim section
and cut 1 in dark green)

Pot rim
(Assemble with the other pot rim section
and cut 1 in dark green)

Front of pot wrap
(Assemble with the other
sections of the pot wrap
and cut 1 in light gray)

Pot base
(cut 2 in
light gray)

**Middle Venus
flytrap pieces**
(cut 1 of each in
light pink)

**Outer Venus
flytrap pieces**
(cut 1 of
each in light
or dark green)

**Back of
pot wrap**
(Assemble
with the other
sections of the
pot wrap and
cut 1 in light
gray)

**Inner Venus
flytrap pieces**
(cut 1 of each
in dark pink)

Venus flytrap leaves
(cut 1 of each in dark or
light green felt)

STICK IT TO THE MAN PINCUSHION

Disheartened by some people's attitudes toward women? Discouraged by reports of sexual harassment? Experience some catharsis and keep your pins close to hand with this pincushion.

YOU WILL NEED

1 piece of light tan felt, 7" x 12" (17.8 x 30.5 cm)

1 piece of yellow felt, 4" x 5" (10.2 x 12.7 cm)

1 piece of navy felt, 3" x 4" (7.6 x 10.2 cm)

1 piece of white felt, 1½" x 2" (3.8 x 5.1 cm)

1 piece of black felt, 1" x 2½" (2.5 x 6.4 cm)

1 piece of dark gray felt, 1½" x 2" (3.8 x 5.1 cm)

1 piece of red felt, 1" x 1" (2.5 x 2.5 cm)

Embroidery floss: black, white, dark gray, yellow, red, navy, and light tan

1 handful polyester fiberfill stuffing

TOOLS

Paper scissors

Sticky tape

Sewing scissors

Embroidery needles

STITCHES

Backstitch (page 21)

Running stitch (page 21)

Overcast stitch (page 23)

DIFFICULTY LEVEL

Intermediate

FINISHED SIZE

4" x 6½" (10.2 x 16.5 cm)

GETTING STARTED

1 Photocopy the pattern pieces on page 111 and cut them out.

2 Tape the paper pattern pieces to the felt, but avoid taping over any stitch detail marks **(A)**:

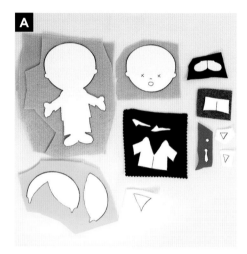

- The head and two body pieces on light tan felt

- The hair on yellow felt

- The suit jacket and lapels on navy felt

- The undershirt and collar on white felt

- The shoes on black felt

- The pants on dark gray felt

- The tie and knot on red felt

3 Cut out the felt pieces that do not have any marked stitch details.

Ouch!

ADDING DETAIL

4 Add the stitch details as marked on the paper patterns using a backstitch and 6 strands of embroidery floss as follows:

- Black to sew the eyes, nose, and mouth on the face, and the seam on the pants

- White to sew the detail on the shirt

- Dark gray to sew the details on the shoes

5 Cut out the detail pieces and remove the paper patterns. You can use hot glue to secure the loose thread ends to the back of the felt so that they don't pull through the fabric when you remove the paper.

FINISHING

6 Position the head and hair pieces on one body piece. Using a running stitch and 6 strands of yellow embroidery floss, sew the hair to the head and body through all the layers along the hairline—do not stitch along the top edge **(B)**.

7 Position the undershirt, suit jacket, tie, and knot on the body. Use a running stitch and 6 strands of the embroidery floss listed to attach the clothes to the body:

- Red to sew the tie and tie knot to the undershirt

- White to sew the collar and undershirt to the body

- Navy to join the suit lapels to the suit jacket and to sew the suit jacket along the armholes, lapels, and bottom edge

- Light tan to sew the head onto the body **(C)**

- Dark gray to sew the top and bottom of the suit pants onto the body

- Black to sew the top of the shoes to the body

8 Place the dressed body section on top of the remaining body section and use an overcast stitch and 6 strands of the embroidery floss listed to join the sections together as follows:

- Black to sew around the edge of the shoes

- Gray to sew around the edge of the pants

- Navy to sew around the edge of the suit jacket

- Light tan to sew around the edge of the head, leaving the top open past the ears so that you can insert the stuffing

9 Insert the polyester fiberfill stuffing between the front and back body layers. Push it down to the toes and hands to fill the body generously **(D)**.

10 Use an overcast stitch and 6 strands of yellow embroidery floss to sew the top of the head closed.

PATTERN PIECES

Patterns shown at 70 percent.
Photocopy at 143 percent to enlarge them to full size.

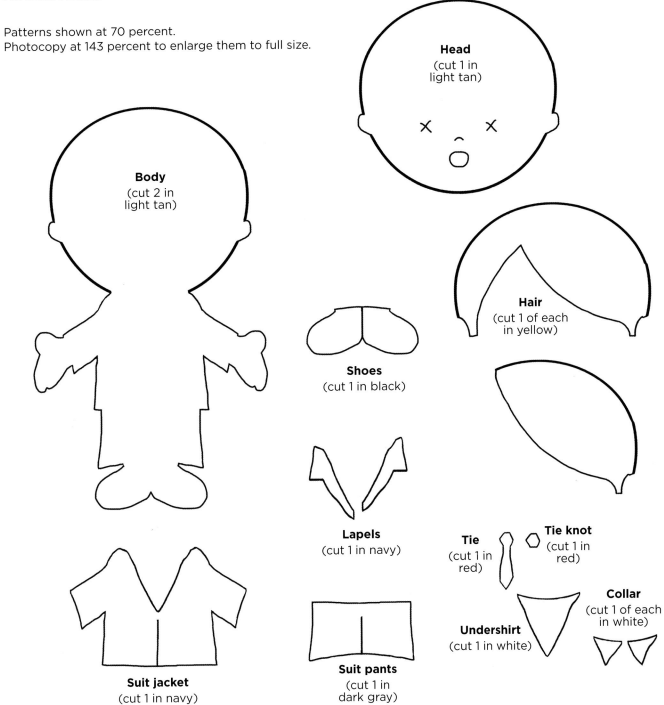

Head
(cut 1 in
light tan)

Body
(cut 2 in
light tan)

Hair
(cut 1 of each
in yellow)

Shoes
(cut 1 in black)

Lapels
(cut 1 in navy)

Tie
(cut 1 in
red)

Tie knot
(cut 1 in
red)

Collar
(cut 1 of each
in white)

Undershirt
(cut 1 in white)

Suit jacket
(cut 1 in navy)

Suit pants
(cut 1 in
dark gray)

PUSSYCAT COFFEE COZY

Grab this pussycat-inspired coffee cozy before you grab your favorite hot beverage. This feisty, eco-friendly feline protects your hands from the heat as you sip and gear up to resist every day.

YOU WILL NEED

1 piece of pink felt, 10″ x 12″ (25.4 x 30.5 cm)

1 piece of white felt, 2″ x 2″ (5.1 x 5.1 cm)

1 piece of gray felt, 1½″ x 1½″ (3.8 x 3.8 cm)

Embroidery floss: pink, light gray, black, and white (or use white sewing thread)

One white hook-and-loop fastener strip, 1¼″ (3 cm) long

TOOLS

Paper scissors

Sticky tape

Sewing scissors

Embroidery needles

Hot glue gun and hot glue sticks

Tweezers

STITCHES

Backstitch (page 21)

French knot (page 25)

Blanket stitch (page 23)

DIFFICULTY LEVEL

Easy

FINISHED SIZE

Approximately 4¼″ x 11½″ (10.8 x 29.2 cm)

GETTING STARTED

1 Photocopy the pattern pieces on page 115 and cut them out.

2 Tape the paper pattern pieces to the felt, but avoid taping over any stitch detail marks **(A)**:

- The front and back base pieces on pink felt

- The inner ear, whites of the eyes, and pupil pieces on white felt

- The nose and iris pieces on gray felt

3 Cut out the felt pieces that do not have any marked stitch details.

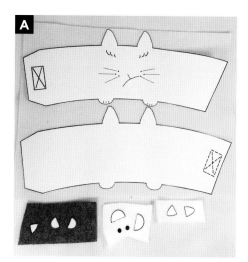

Equal rights for felines!

ADDING DETAILS

4 Add the stitch details as marked on the paper patterns using 6 strands of the embroidery floss listed. Use:

- A backstitch in black to stitch the whiskers, eyelashes, mouth, and paw lines **(B)**

- A French knot in light gray for the whisker dots

5 Cut out the front base piece and remove the paper pattern from the face. Keep the piece with the hook and loop guide to position the hook-and-loop fastener later.

FINISHING

6 Attach the hook-and-loop fasteners using a backstitch and 6 strands of white embroidery floss as follows **(C)**:

- Sew the hook section for the back base piece on the underside of the felt, as shown on the template. (It will not be visible when you set your piece down.)

- Sew the hook section for the front base piece on the top side of the felt as shown on the template.

7 Use a blanket stitch and 6 strands of pink embroidery floss to sew the front and back base pieces together, making sure that the hook-and-loop pieces are positioned correctly. The back piece will be facing down on the right side of the cup cozy; the front piece will be facing up on the left side of the cup cozy.

8 Use hot glue to join the remaining pieces. Use tweezers to hold the felt as you're gluing and placing pieces in this order:

- The ear pieces to the center of the ear shapes on the front base piece

- The nose piece just above the mouth

- The iris and pupil pieces onto the whites of the eye pieces on the front base piece

- The entire eye piece onto the front base piece just below the lashes **(D)**

Feminist Facts

In January 2017, the Women's March on Washington inspired 672 similar events around the world. As a result, nearly 5 million people marched to create transformative social change! They demanded reproductive, LGBTQIA, civil, disability, workers', and immigrants' rights, environmental justice, as well as an end to violence. Many of them wore hand-knitted "pussy hats"—pink hats with ears. They were the brainchild of Hollywood screenwriter and feminist Krista Suh and Kat Coyle, who runs The Little Knittery yarn store in Los Feliz Village, Los Angeles, CA.

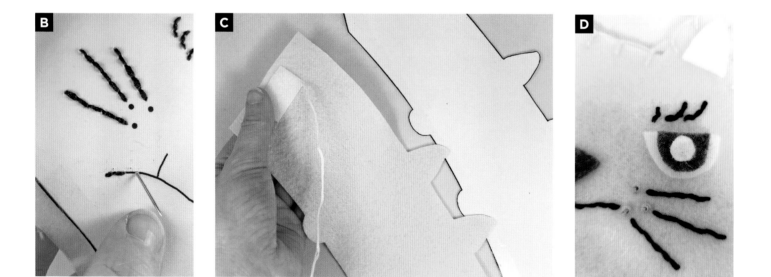

PATTERN PIECES

Patterns shown at 60 percent. Photocopy at 167 percent to enlarge them to full size.

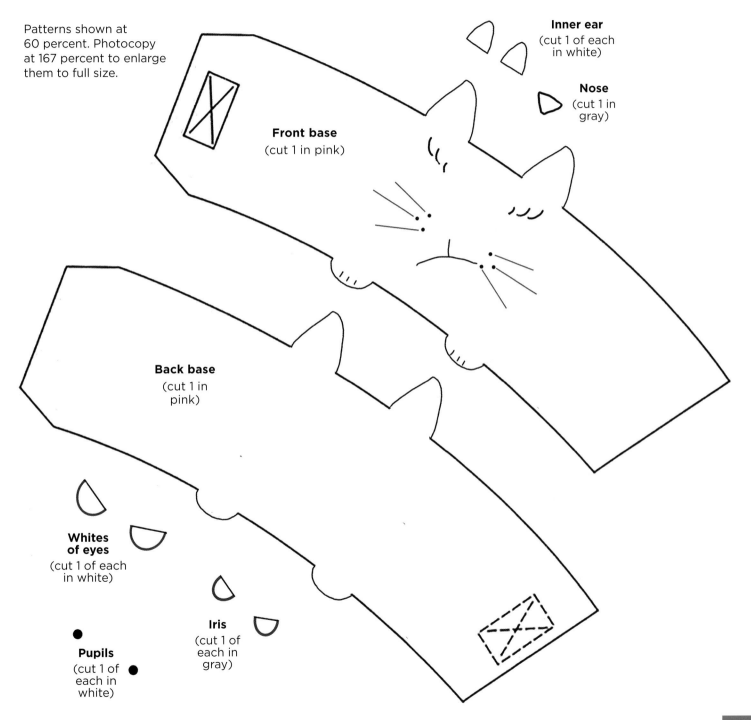

Inner ear
(cut 1 of each in white)

Nose
(cut 1 in gray)

Front base
(cut 1 in pink)

Back base
(cut 1 in pink)

Whites of eyes
(cut 1 of each in white)

Iris
(cut 1 of each in gray)

Pupils
(cut 1 of each in white)

LITTLE FLOWER TAMPON ROLL

This roll holds tampons and pads so you can find your feminine hygiene products when you need them. Keep your supplies next to a yellow rose —a symbol of the suffragette movement.

YOU WILL NEED

1 piece of dark gray felt, 9½" x 17" (24.1 x 43.2 cm)

1 piece of yellow felt, 8" x 9" (20.3 x 22.9 cm)

Embroidery floss: medium brown, yellow, and dark gray

One ⅛-inch (3 mm) grommet

One length of leather cord, 14" (35.6 cm)

TOOLS

Paper scissors

Sticky tape

Sewing scissors

Embroidery needles

Hot glue gun and hot glue sticks

Grommet kit and hammer

STITCHES

Backstitch (page 21)

Running Stitch (page 21)

DIFFICULTY LEVEL

Easy

FINISHED SIZE

7¾" x 9" (19.7 x 22.9 cm) open

7¾" x 3" (19.7 x 7.6 cm) closed

GETTING STARTED

1 Photocopy the pattern pieces on page 119 and cut them out.

2 Tape the paper pattern pieces to the felt, but avoid taping over any stitch detail marks **(A)**:

- The cover and lining of the roll on dark gray felt

- The pocket, flap, and tab closure pieces on yellow felt

3 Cut out all the felt pieces except for the lining piece. Tape the front pattern to the felt to hold it in place while you embroider it. Cut holes into your tab closures where marked.

ADDING DETAIL

4 Add the stitch details as marked on the paper patterns using 6 strands of the embroidery floss listed. Use:

- A backstitch in medium brown to embroider the vine on the roll lining **(B)**
- A backstitch in yellow to embroider the rose onto the roll lining

5 Cut out the lining. Carefully remove the paper pattern. You can use hot glue to secure the loose thread ends to the back of the felt so that they don't pull through the fabric when you remove the paper.

FINISHING

6 Use a backstitch and 6 strands of dark gray embroidery floss to attach the inner pocket to the tampon roll lining. Following the stitching lines on the pattern, only sew the inside detail of the pocket onto the lining. Do not sew onto the cover—you will join it in the next step.

7 With all the layers together (flap, lining, and cover), use a running stitch and 6 strands of dark gray embroidery floss to attach the flap to the top left of the cover and lining pieces. Continue sewing around the edge of the roll, including the left and bottom edges of the pocket.

8 Position the tab closures back-to-back at the center of the short edge without the pocket—one below the cover and one on top of the lining of the roll **(C)**. Use a dab of hot glue to hold the tabs together in the center. Use a running stitch and 6 strands of dark gray embroidery floss to sew along the edges of the tab closures and attach them to each other and the tampon roll.

9 Following the package instructions, use the grommet kit to affix the grommet to the tab closure and reinforce the holes made in step 3 **(D)**. Tie the leather cord through the grommet and use to close the tampon roll.

> **"Freedom is always the freedom of dissenters."**
>
> **–Rosa Luxemburg**

PATTERN PIECES

Patterns shown at 40 percent.
Photocopy at 250 percent to enlarge them to full size.

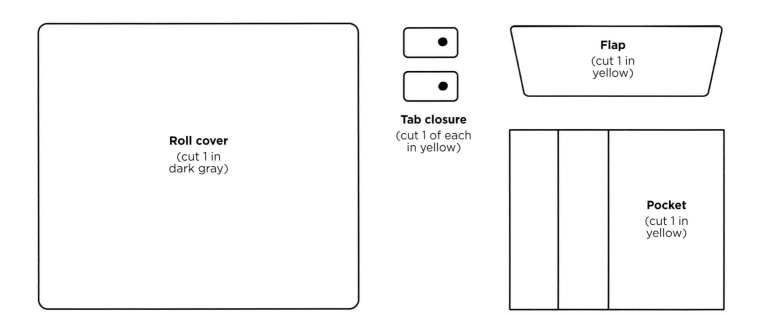

Roll cover
(cut 1 in
dark gray)

Tab closure
(cut 1 of each
in yellow)

Flap
(cut 1 in
yellow)

Pocket
(cut 1 in
yellow)

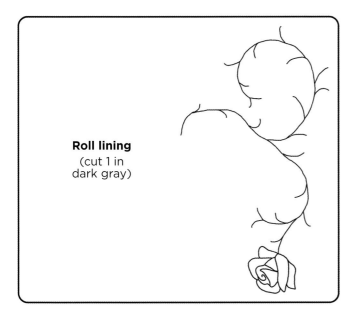

Roll lining
(cut 1 in
dark gray)

Feminist Facts

In some parts of developing countries, sanitary products are scarce and menstruation is a taboo topic. During their periods, many girls stay home from school because they don't have pads or tampons to use. They skip school as a result and sometimes are socially stigmatized too. In response, international charities have launched campaigns to teach women about their bodies and debunk the harmful superstitions that surround menstruation. Through public donations, charities like 50 Cents.Period., Femme International, and Dignity Period work with young women on the ground, helping them stay in school, supplying them with reusable sanitary products, and giving them the tools they need to have autonomy over their bodies.

LABRYS BARRETTES

The two-headed labrys ax has represented feminine strength and solidarity since the 1970s. Adorn your hair with this fierce pair of matriarchal symbols.

YOU WILL NEED

For the embroidered barrette:
1 piece of light blue felt, 6″ x 6″ (15.2 x 15.2 cm)
Embroidery floss: brown, dark gray, light gray, and light blue
One 2-inch (5.1 cm) metal barrette

For the simple barrette:
1 piece of dark gray felt, 3″ x 4″ (7.6 x 10.2 cm)
1 piece of brown felt, 1″ x 2.5″ (2.5 x 6.4 cm)
1 piece of purple felt, 3″ x 3.5″ (7.6 x 8.9 cm)
One 2-inch (5.1 cm) metal barrette
Embroidery floss: purple and dark gray

TOOLS

Paper scissors
Sticky tape
Sewing scissors
Embroidery needles
Hot glue gun and hot glue sticks

STITCHES

Backstitch (page 21)
Split stitch (page 24)
Satin stitch (page 24)
Long and short shading stitch (page 25)
Overcast stitch (page 23)
Running stitch (page 21)

DIFFICULTY LEVEL

Intermediate (embroidered barrette) and easy (simple barrette)

FINISHED SIZE

Embroidered barrette: 2¼″ x 3″ (5.7 x 7.6 cm)
Simple barrette: 2¼″ x 2½″(5.7 x 6.4 cm)

GETTING STARTED

1 Photocopy the pattern pieces on page 123 and cut them out.

2 Tape the paper pattern pieces to the felt, but avoid taping over any stitch detail marks:

- For the embroidered barrette, the two base fronts, and top and bottom pocket pieces on light blue felt **(A)**

- For the simple barrette, the two ax head pieces on dark gray felt, the ax handle on brown felt, and the base back piece and both end pocket pieces on purple felt

3 Cut out the felt pieces that do not have any marked stitch details.

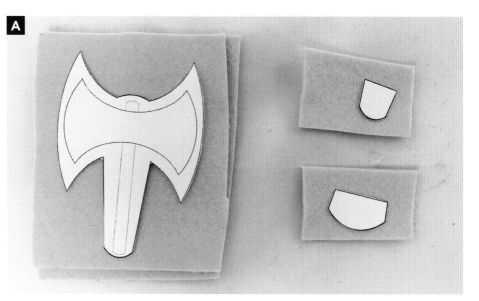

A

ADDING DETAIL

4 Start to add the stitch details to the embroidered barrette following the outline marked on the paper pattern and using the number of strands of embroidery floss as follows:

- A backstitch in brown (3 strands) to stitch the handle outline

- A split stitch in dark gray (4 strands) to stitch the ax head outline **(B)**

5 Cut out the base front and remove the paper pattern. You can use hot glue to secure the loose thread ends to the back of the felt so that they don't pull through the fabric when you remove the paper.

6 Embroider the ax details on the base front. With 6 strands of floss, use a satin stitch in brown to fill in the handle detail and a satin stitch in dark gray to fill in the center of the ax head. Use a long and short shading stitch and dark gray to fill in the ax head, starting each stitch from the center of the ax and ending slightly outside the ax head outline. When you get close to the edge of the blade, switch to light gray floss, and use the long and short shading stitch to blend the light gray with the dark gray. The stitches should end just outside the outline of the blades. Work the different colored stitches side by side rather than overlap them **(C)**.

FINISHING

7 To begin assembling the embroidered barrette, use a backstitch and 6 strands of light blue embroidery floss to attach the sides of the top pocket to the base back.

8 Stack all three layers (front, base back, and pockets) together. Use an overcast stitch and 6 strands of light blue embroidery floss to stitch them together around the perimeter, taking care not to stitch closed the pocket layers facing the inside of the barrette. They will be used to hold the metal barrette.

9 Slip the barrette into the pockets of the embroidered barrette **(D)**.

10 To begin assembling the simple barrette, use a running stitch and 6 strands of purple embroidery floss to stitch along the perimeter of the base back to attach the pocket pieces to the base back.

11 Place the ax handle in between the two ax head pieces and use an overcast stitch and 6 strands of dark gray embroidery floss to sew the two ax head pieces together.

12 Glue the finished labrys onto the front of the purple barrette piece (on the side without the pockets) **(E)**.

13 Slip the ends of the metal barrette into the pockets of the simple barrette.

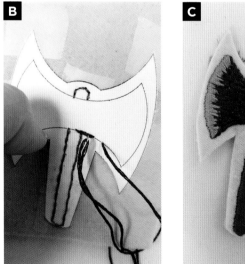

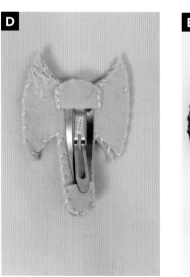

PATTERN PIECES

Patterns shown true to size.
Photocopy at 100 percent.

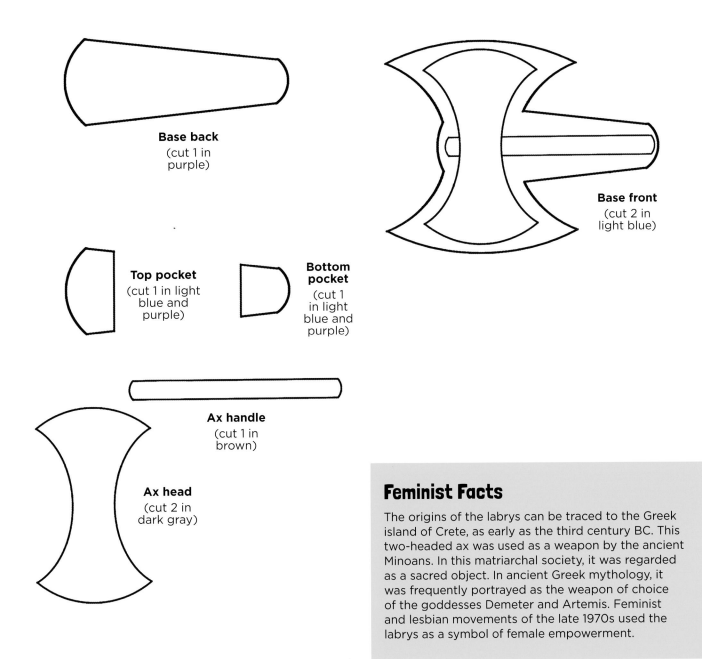

Base back
(cut 1 in purple)

Base front
(cut 2 in light blue)

Top pocket
(cut 1 in light blue and purple)

Bottom pocket
(cut 1 in light blue and purple)

Ax handle
(cut 1 in brown)

Ax head
(cut 2 in dark gray)

Feminist Facts

The origins of the labrys can be traced to the Greek island of Crete, as early as the third century BC. This two-headed ax was used as a weapon by the ancient Minoans. In this matriarchal society, it was regarded as a sacred object. In ancient Greek mythology, it was frequently portrayed as the weapon of choice of the goddesses Demeter and Artemis. Feminist and lesbian movements of the late 1970s used the labrys as a symbol of female empowerment.

RESOURCES

BRICKS–AND–MORTAR STORES

USA

Jo-Ann Fabric and Craft Stores
joann.com

Michaels
michaels.com

Blick Art Materials
dickblick.com

A.C. Moore
acmoore.com

Artist & Craftsman Supply
artistcraftsman.com

UK

Hobbycraft
hobbycraft.co.uk

Abakhan
abakhan.co.uk

The Makery
Bath, UK; themakery.co.uk

Craft and More
Bristol, UK; craftandmore.co.uk

Fred Aldous
Manchester, UK; fredaldous.co.uk

Anycraft-UK
Kidderminster, UK; anycraftuk.co.uk

ONLINE STORES

USA

Amazon
amazon.com

American Felt and Craft
feltandcraft.com

CraftSubversive
etsy.com/shop/CraftSubversive

The Felt Store
thefeltstore.com

Fabric.com
fabric.com

UK

Amazon
amazon.co.uk

Cloud Craft
cloudcraft.co.uk

Blooming Felt
bloomingfelt.co.uk

Willow Fabrics
willowfabrics.com

Minerva Crafts
minervacrafts.com

Home Crafts
homecrafts.co.uk

ACKNOWLEDGMENTS

I'd like to thank:

Derrick and Nadia for their patience, support, and assistance (and non-assistance).

My sister for being my sounding board and brainstorming partner.

My parents for being benevolently confused by my various projects.

Also, the MTJMs for their enthusiasm and encouragement.

Special thanks to the great team at Toucan: Sarah Bloxham, Julie Brooke, Ellen Dupont, and Leah Germann.

PICTURE CREDITS

All images taken by Missy Covington (© Toucan Books Ltd.) except:

iStock: © czarny_bez: 12; © Floortje: 10 (top right); © malerapaso: 10 (top left); © mrkob: 11 (bottom right); © sutteerug: 11 (left); © rusm: 5, 9, 27, 49, 75, 103, 125, back cover

Headings set in Londrina. Designed by Marcelo Magalhães Pereira (marcelomagalhaes.net) and licensed under a Creative Commons Attribution ShareAlike license.

INDEX